Hot C

Rebecca Jad

methuen | drama

LONDON • NEW YORK • OXFORD • NEW DELHI • SYDNEY

METHUEN DRAMA
Bloomsbury Publishing Plc, 50 Bedford Square, London, WC1B 3DP, UK
Bloomsbury Publishing Inc, 1385 Broadway, New York, NY 10018, USA
Bloomsbury Publishing Ireland, 29 Earlsfort Terrace, Dublin 2,
D02 AY28, Ireland

BLOOMSBURY, METHUEN DRAMA and the Methuen
Drama logo are trademarks of Bloomsbury Publishing Plc.

First published in Great Britain 2025

Copyright © Rebecca Jade Hammond, 2025

Rebecca Jade Hammond has asserted their right under the Copyright,
Designs and Patents Act, 1988, to be identified as Author of this work.

For legal purposes the Acknowledgements on p. xvi-xvii
constitute an extension of this copyright page.

Cover design: Kelly King

Cover image: Kirsten McTernan

All rights reserved. No part of this publication may be: i) reproduced or transmitted in any form, electronic or mechanical, including photocopying, recording or by means of any information storage or retrieval system without prior permission in writing from the publishers; or ii) used or reproduced in any way for the training, development or operation of artificial intelligence (AI) technologies, including generative AI technologies. The rights holders expressly reserve this publication from the text and data mining exception as per Article 4(3) of the Digital Single Market Directive (EU) 2019/790.

Bloomsbury Publishing Plc does not have any control over, or responsibility for, any third-party websites referred to or in this book. All internet addresses given in this book were correct at the time of going to press. The author and publisher regret any inconvenience caused if addresses have changed or sites have ceased to exist, but can accept no responsibility for any such changes.

No rights in incidental music or songs contained in the work are hereby granted and performance rights for any performance/presentation whatsoever must be obtained from the respective copyright owners.

All rights whatsoever in this play are strictly reserved and application for performance etc. should be made before rehearsals begin to The Haworth Agency, Studio 103, Babel Studios, 158b Kentish Town Road, London, NW5 2AG (permissions@haworthagency.co.uk). No performance may be given unless a licence has been obtained.

A catalogue record for this book is available from the British Library.

Library of Congress Control Number: 2025932892

ISBN: PB: 978-1-3505-5969-1
ePDF: 978-1-3505-5970-7
eBook: 978-1-3505-5971-4

Series: Modern Plays

Typeset by Mark Heslington Ltd, Scarborough, North Yorkshire
Printed and bound in Great Britain.

For product safety related questions contact
productsafety@bloomsbury.com.

To find out more about our authors and books visit
www.bloomsbury.com and sign up for our newsletters.

HOT CHICKS

Cast

Kyla **Izzi McCormack John**
Ruby **Londiwe Mthembu**
Cheney **Richard Elis**
Sadie **Rachel Redford**

Creative Team / Tîm Creadigol

Writer / Ysgrifennwr **Rebecca Jade Hammond**
Director / Cyfarwyddwr **Hannah Noone**
Assistant Director / Cyfarwyddwr Cynorthwyol **Dena Davies**
Designer / Cynllunydd **Hannah Wolfe**
Lighting Designer / Cynllunydd Goleuo **Katy Morison**
Sound Designer / Cynllunydd Sain **Tic Ashfield**
Fight Director / Cyfarwyddwr Ymladd **Kevin McCurdy**
Wellbeing Coach / Hyfforddwr Lles **Ndidi John**
Dramaturg **Davina Moss**

Production Team / Tîm Cynhyrchu

Production Manager / Rheolwr Cynhyrchu **Mandy Ivory-Castile**
Company Stage Manager / Rheolwr Llwyfan y Cwmni **Josh Miles**
Deputy Stage Manager / Dirprwy Reolwr Llwyfan **Emily Howard**
Assistant Stage Manager / Rheolwr Llwyfan Cynorthwyol **Lizzie Welsh**
Technical Manager / Rheolwr Technegol **Rachel Mortimer**
Technicians / Technegwyr **Ruby James, Charlie Moore, Hollie Morrison, James Tomlinson**
Costume Supervisor / Goruchwyliwr Gwisgoedd **Nikita Verboon**
Construction / Adeiladwaith **Matt Carter, Will Hawkins**
Scenic Artists / Artistiaid Golygfaol **Emily Jones, Kayleigh Smith**

Hot Chicks was first performed on 21 March 2025 at Sherman Theatre
Perfformiwyd *Hot Chicks* am y tro cyntaf ar 21 Mawrth 2025 yn Theatr y Sherman

Sherman Cymru Productions Ltd | Registered Charity Number / Rhif Elusen Cofrestredig 1118364

MAKING THEATRE IS A TEAM EFFORT. IT REQUIRES A BROAD RANGE OF SKILLS AND EXPERTISE TO MAKE A PRODUCTION HAPPEN. THIS IS THE SHERMAN TEAM: / GWAITH TÎM YW CREU THEATR. MAE GOFYN AM YSTOD EANG O SGILIAU AC ARBENIGEDD I GREU CYNHYRCHIAD. DYMA DÎM Y SHERMAN:

Executive / Gweithredol

Chief Executive / Prif Weithredwr
Julia Barry

Artistic Administration
Gweinyddiaeth Artistig

Producing and Programming Manager / Rheolwr Cynhyrchu a Rhaglennu
Patricia O'Sullivan

Creative Engagement
Ymgysylltu Creadigol

Creative Engagement Manager
Rheolwr Ymgysylltu Creadigol
Francesca Pickard

Creative Engagement Assistant (Interim) / Cynorthwyydd Ymgysylltu Creadigol (Dros Dro)
Cerys Grail

Finance and Administration
Cyllid a Gweinyddiaeth

Head of Finance and Administration
Pennaeth Cyllid a Gweinyddiaeth
Sally Shepherd

Company Administrator / Gweinyddwr Cwmni **Helen Macintyre**

Finance and Administration Assistant
Cynorthwyydd Cyllid a Gweinyddiaeth
Mikey Porter

Front of House / Blaen y Tŷ

Head of Operations / Pennaeth Gweithrediadau **Kevin Burt**

Bar and Kitchen Manager / Rheolwr y Bar a'r Gegin **Anne Marie Saunders**

Visitor Experience Manager
Rheolwr Profiad Ymwelwyr
Roisin Miller O'Brien

Bar and Kitchen Supervisor
Goruchwyliwr y Bar a'r Gegin
Ben Moruzzi

Bar and Kitchen Assistants
Cynorthwywyr Bar a Chegin
Alexander Prime, Cata Lindegaard, Chloe Parkes, Enfys Macmillan, Gethin Roberts, Glain Llwyd, Huw Ferguson, Isobelle Tischler, Joel Edwards, Katie Dobbins, Macsen McKay, Megan Featherstone, Scarlett Morley, Theo Greenwood

Fundraising and Development
Codi Arian a Datblygu

Head of Fundraising and Development
Pennaeth Codi Arian a Datblygu
Emma Tropman

Literary / Llenyddol

Literary Manager / Rheolwr Llenyddol
Davina Moss

Literary Associate / Cydymaith Llenyddol **Lowri Morgan**

Marketing and Communications
Marchnata a Chyfathrebu

Head of Marketing and Communications / Pennaeth Marchnata a Chyfathrebu
Ed Newsome

Box Office and Audience Insight Manager / Rheolwr y Swyddfa Docynnau a Mewnwelediadau Cynulleidfaoedd
Caroline Carter

Press Manager (Freelance)
Rheolwr y Wasg (Llawrydd)
Catrin Rogers

Box Office Supervisors
Goruchwylwyr y Swyddfa Docynnau
Menna Chandler, Charla Grace

Box Office Assistants / Cynorthwywyr y Swyddfa Docynnau **Bella Crowne, Poppy Damazer, Joel Edwards, Karen Kisakye, Helen Morgan, Louise Nichols, Gethin Roberts, Bethany Williams-Potter, Bob Tharme**

Production and Planning
Cynhyrchu a Chynllunio

Head of Production and Planning
Pennaeth Cynhyrchu a Chynllunio
Mandy Ivory-Castile

Company Stage Manager / Rheolwr Llwyfan y Cwmni **Josh Miles**

Technical Manager / Rheolwr Technegol **Rachel Mortimer**

Thank you to our incredible Volunteer Ushers: / Diolch yn fawr i'n Tywyswyr Gwirfoddol anhygoel:
Abbas Radaideh, Ali Robinson, Alyssa Aziz, Amy Woods, Anna Lam, Anne Wei, Arabella Foster, Archie Beaumont- Denning, Ben Ping, Charles Gabe, Chloe Parkes, Chris Harvey, Clive Rudge, Clive Ward, Dana Tait, Dave Webb, David Jones, David Prew, Debbie Chapman, Dylan Chichester, Eileen Leahy, Emily Allan, Eva Leslie, Fiona McDonald, Germaine Walsh, Grace Uruski, Hannah Quinn, Helen Rankmore, Irina Guliaeva, Jen Sutton, Jenny Cripps, Kate McCann, Katie Brown, Kevin Chubb, Kirsty Campbell, Leah Kerr, Lizzie Moreland, Lucia Taher, Lucinda Devine, Magdalena Sowka, Maicon Delarmelina, Mair Bevan, Maram Almolliyeh, Martin Gray, Mary Prew, Mary Rudge, Matthew Bedford, Mehdi Razi, Mike Jones, Nick Fisk, Paige Cooper, Paul Mitchell, Peter Gaskell, Radu Harnu, Rebecca Grey, Rhydian Waters, Rhys Evans, Rubie Follon, Sean Parker, Sian Davies, Stephanie Campbell, Sue Hayes, Terri Delahunty, Theo Greenwood, Tom Powell, Tom Rhys, Tony Wu, Vittoria Ferrari, Zeljka Whittaker

---

BOARD OF TRUSTEES
YMDDIRIEDOLWYR
Ceri Davies
(Chair / Cadeirydd)
Rhian Head
(Vice Chair / Is-gadeirydd)
**Llinos Daniel
Lauren Hamilton
Alex Hicks
Darren Joyce
Ifty Khan
Janice Lane
Márta Minier
Marc Simcox
Huw Thomas
Louise Thomas
Roger Tomlinson
Jane Tyler
Helen Vallis**

GRAND AMBITION IS A CREATIVE COLLECTIVE MADE UP OF: / MAE UCHELGAIS GRAND YN GYDWEITHFA GREADIGOL SY'N CYNNWYS:

**Steve Balsamo
Michelle McTernan
Richard Mylan
Christian Patterson**

On Hot Chicks for Grand Ambition:
Ar Hot Chicks ar gyfer Uchelgais Grand:

Co Producers / Cynhyrchwyr ar y cyd
Michelle McTernan & Richard Mylan

Fundraising, Marketing & PR / Codi Arian, Marchnata a Chysylltiadau Cyhoeddus **Stella Patrick**

With special thanks to / Gyda diolch arbennig i: **Dr Nina Maxwell, CMET Swansea's Young People's Panel, and the young people of YHub**

WELCOME FROM SHERMAN THEATRE
CROESO GAN THEATR Y SHERMAN

Rebecca is one of the boldest and most distinctive voices in Welsh theatre. Therefore, we are incredibly proud to be producing the premiere of her fierce new play with our friends at Grand Ambition. Both Sherman Theatre and Grand Ambition are focussed on sharing compelling and important south Wales stories with our audiences, so we knew there could be no better partner to present *Hot Chicks* with than Grand Ambition.

Hot Chicks is the definition of a local story that speaks to the world. Rebecca's play is both unnerving and funny; an unflinching look at the young women trapped by criminal exploitation. It does what great new writing should do, it demands that we think about the world around us and see that world through the eyes of others.

Mae Rebecca yn un o leisiau mwyaf beiddgar a mwyaf nodedig y theatr yng Nghymru. Felly, rydym yn hynod o falch o fod yn cynhyrchu'r perfformiadau cyntaf o'i drama newydd ffyrnig gyda'n ffrindiau yn Grand Ambition. Mae Theatr y Sherman a Grand Ambition yn canolbwyntio ar rannu straeon cymhellol a phwysig o dde Cymru gyda'n cynulleidfaoedd, felly gwyddem nad oes gwell partner i gyflwyno *Hot Chicks* na Grand Ambition.

Mae *Hot Chicks* yn enghraifft berffaith o stori leol sy'n siarad â'r byd. Mae drama Rebecca yn frawychus ac yn ddoniol; yn rhoi cipolwg cadarn ar y merched ifanc sy'n cael eu caethiwo gan gam-fanteisio troseddol. Mae'n cyflawni'r hyn y dylai ysgrifennu newydd craff ei wneud, mae'n mynnu ein bod yn ystyried y byd o'n cwmpas a gweld y byd hwnnw trwy lygaid eraill.

Julia Barry
Chief Executive / Prif Weithredwr

WELCOME FROM GRAND AMBITION
CROESO GAN UCHELGAIS GRAND

Since we founded Grand Ambition with the support of Swansea Council three years ago, we've been committed to creating world-class theatre for all of Swansea's communities, not just those with a history of theatre-going; nurturing and retaining homegrown creative talent to tell the stories that matter to our city.

It is important to us to tell the stories of marginalised people, representing voices less frequently heard on our stages. To be able to join forces with Sherman Theatre to tell a powerful story, with Rebecca Jade Hammond's razor-sharp script is such a brilliant opportunity.

For all the attention child criminal exploitation is getting at the moment, there's been very little in the media that gives voice to the young people affected. Rebecca's script does just that – these are very human characters, you can't help but be swept along with them. Alongside the play we've been working with young people via Social Services and YMCA to ensure they feel heard and to help us get accurate and useful information out to schools all across Wales, thanks to support from Arts Council Wales and continued support from Swansea Council.

Ers i ni sefydlu Uchelgais Grand gyda chymorth Cyngor Abertawe dair blynedd yn ôl, rydym wedi ein hymrwymo i greu theatr o safon fyd-eang ar gyfer holl gymunedau Abertawe, nid dim ond rheiny sydd wedi arfer â mynychu'r theatr; i feithrin a chadw talent greadigol leol i adrodd y straeon sy'n bwysig i'n dinas.

Mae'n bwysig i ni adrodd straeon pobl a ymyleiddiwyd, gan gynrychioli lleisiau sydd ddim yn cael eu clywed mor aml ar ein llwyfannau. Mae cydweithio â Theatr y Sherman i adrodd stori mor bwerus, gyda sgript graff Rebecca Jade Hammond, yn gyfle gwych.

Er bod camfanteisio troseddol ar blant yn cael tipyn o sylw ar hyn o bryd, bach iawn sydd yn y cyfryngau sy'n rhoi llais i'r bobl ifanc sy'n cael eu heffeithio. Dyma'n union y mae sgript Rebecca yn ei wneud – mae'r cymeriadau hyn yn ddynol iawn, ac anodd iawn yw peidio â chwympo i ganol eu stori. Ynghyd â'r ddrama, rydym wedi bod yn gweithio gyda phobl ifanc trwy Wasanaethau Cymdeithasol ac YMCA i sicrhau eu bod yn teimlo eu bod yn cael eu clywed ac i'n helpu ni i rannu gwybodaeth gywir a ddefnyddiol ag ysgolion ledled Cymru, diolch i gefnogaeth Cyngor Celfyddydau Cymru a chefnogaeth barhaus gan Gyngor Abertawe.

NOTE FROM THE WRITER
NODYN GAN YR YSGRIFENNWR
Rebecca Jade Hammond

I became aware of the crisis of county lines and grooming during the pandemic. There was a spike in children being groomed across the UK, drug running across the borders of England and Wales in light of schools being closed and education being taken online. In recent years, government cuts to youth clubs, community centres and closing of parks have made vulnerable young people easy targets for organised crime networks who prey on them and coax them into serious crime rings. More recently, there has been an increase in girls and young women playing key roles and it is those women I wanted to put front and centre into this new piece of Welsh theatre. My research on this project over the last five years has deepened my understanding of the socio-political issues surrounding the county line crisis (especially in Wales) and the need for vital action, funding and protections put in place to stop young people being drawn into these drug networks. Once you are indoctrinated into these almost cult-like organisations, it is very hard to have the strength to leave because of the fear of putting your family or yourself in danger. *Hot Chicks* is a play about those young girls who fall through the cracks of education and society, forgotten and just looking for familial support and safety.

Des i'n fwy ymwybodol o argyfwng y llinellau cyffuriau a meithrin perthynas amhriodol yn ystod y pandemig. Roedd twf mawr yn yr achosion o feithrin perthynas amhriodol â phlant ledled y DU er mwyn symud cyffuriau dros y ffin rhwng Cymru a Lloegr, a hyn yn sgil cau ysgolion a symud addysg ar-lein. Yn ystod y blynyddoedd diwethaf, mae toriadau Llywodraethol ar glybiau ieuenctid, canolfannau cymunedol a chau parciau wedi gwneud pobl ifanc bregus yn dargedau hawdd i rwydweithiau troseddu cyfundrefnol, sy'n eu hannog i ymuno â grwpiau troseddu difrifol. Yn fwy diweddar, mae'r nifer o ferched a menywod ifanc sy'n chwarae rhannau allweddol wedi cynyddu, a'r merched hyn yr oeddwn eisiau rhoi ar flaen llwyfan yn y darn newydd hwn o theatr Gymreig. Mae fy ymchwil ar y prosiect hwn dros y pum mlynedd diwethaf wedi dwyn fy nealltwriaeth o'r materion cymdeithasol a gwleidyddol sy'n amgylchynu'r argyfwng llinellau cyffuriau (yn enwedig yng Nghymru) a'r angen i roi ar waith cynllun gweithredu, cyllid a diogelwch i atal pobl ifanc rhag cael eu tynnu i mewn i'r rhwydweithiau cyffuriau hyn. Unwaith mae rhywun yn cael ei dynnu i mewn i'r cyfundrefnau defod hyn, mae'n anodd iawn cael y nerth i adael oherwydd y gofid o roi'ch teulu neu eich hun mewn perygl. Mae *Hot Chicks* yn ddrama am ferched ifanc sy'n syrthio trwy afael addysg a chymdeithas, wedi'u hanghofio ac sy'n chwilio am gefnogaeth deuluol a diogelwch.

CARDIFF'S THEATRE FOR WALES

Imagine a world made more equitable, more compassionate, more unified by the power of theatre. We are driven to achieve this vision every day. We do this by creating and curating shared live theatre experiences that inspire people from all backgrounds across South Wales to make a better world, in their own way. We believe that access to creativity and self-expression is a right and we constantly strive to ensure everyone has the opportunity to be enriched by the art of theatre.

Our focus on the development and production of new writing and on nurturing Welsh and Wales-based artists makes us the engine room of Welsh theatre. We tell Welsh stories with global resonance through our Made at Sherman productions, created under our roof right here in the heart of Cardiff. We're a place for everyone, generating opportunities for the citizens of South Wales to connect with theatre through inspiring and visionary engagement.

THEATR I GYMRU YNG NGHAERDYDD

Dychmygwch fyd lle gall pŵer y theatr greu byd tecach, mwy tosturiol ac unedig. Cawn ein hysgogi i gyflawni'r weledigaeth yma yn ddyddiol. Rydyn ni'n gwneud hyn drwy greu a churadu profiadau theatr byw i'w rhannu ac i ysbrydoli pobl o bob cefndir ar draws De Cymru i fedru gwneud byd gwell, yn eu ffordd eu hunain. Credwn fod pawb â'r hawl i gael mynediad at greadigrwydd a hunanfynegiant, ac ymdrechwn yn gyson i sicrhau bod pawb yn cael y cyfle i gael eu cyfoethogi gan y theatr.

Mae ein ffocws ar ddatblygu a chynhyrchu gwaith newydd ac ar feithrin artistiaid Cymraeg ac o Gymru yn ein gwneud ni'n injan i fyd y theatr yng Nghymru. Trwy ein cynyrchiadau Crëwyd yn y Sherman, rydym yn adrodd straeon Cymraeg sy'n cyseinio negeseuon o bwys yn fyd-eang, a chaiff pob un eu creu o dan ein to yng nghalon Caerdydd. Rydym yn le i bawb, gan greu cyfleoedd i bobl De Cymru gysylltu â'r theatr drwy ymrwymiad ysbrydoledig a gweledigaethol.

SHERMAN THEATRE IS A REGISTERED CHARITY.
Donate today to help to secure our future.

MAE THEATR Y SHERMAN YN ELUSEN GOFRESTREDIG.
Cyfrannwch heddiw i helpu i sicrhau ein dyfodol.

SHERMANTHEATRE.CO.UK

Sherman Cymru Productions Ltd | Registered Charity Number / Rhif Elusen Gofrestredig 1118364

GRAND AMBITION TELLS SWANSEA STORIES.

This dynamic theatre company is committed to nurturing and retaining homegrown creative talent, telling stories that matter to and resonate with the people of Swansea and beyond. The company was established in 2021 by creatives Richard Mylan, Michelle McTernan, Steve Balsamo and Christian Patterson in partnership with Swansea Council to become the resident producing and community engagement company at the city's Swansea Grand Theatre and Brangwyn Hall; a partnership which continues as Grand Ambition develops as a project funded community interest company. Their first production *Sorter* earned writer Richard Mylan a Stage Debut award nomination and was listed in The Stage 50 Best Shows of 2023. Their 2024 production, *MumFighter* by Tracy Harris, was listed in The Stage 50 Best Shows of 2024. Both productions earned a raft of 4 & 5 Star reviews. The company received the inaugural Arts & Business Cymru Hodge Foundation Arts Award in 2024.

MAE UCHELGAIS GRAND YN ADRODD STRAEON ABERTAWE.

Mae'r cwmni theatr dynamig hwn wedi ymrwymo i feithrin a chadw talent greadigol leol, gan greu straeon sy'n bwysig ac sy'n uniaethu â phobl Abertawe a thu hwnt. Sefydlwyd y cwmni yn 2021 gan yr unigolion creadigol Richard Mylan, Michelle McTernan, Steve Balsamo a Christian Patterson mewn partneriaeth â Chyngor Abertawe, i weithio fel y cwmni cynhyrchu ac ymgysylltu cymunedol breswyl yn Theatr y Grand Abertawe a Neuadd Brangwyn; partneriaeth sydd yn parhau wrth i Uchelgais Grand ddatblygu fel cwmni buddiant cymunedol a ariannwyd gan brosiectau. Trwy eu cynhyrchiad cyntaf *Sorter*, cafodd y dramodydd Richard Mylan enwebiad am wobr y Stage Debut, a chafodd y ddrama ei rhestru ar restr The Stage am y 50 sioe orau yn 2023. Cafodd eu cynhyrchiad yn 2024, *MumFighter* gan Tracy Harris, ei restru ar restr The Stage am y 50 sioe orau yn 2024. Enillodd y ddau gynhyrchiad nifer o adolygiadau 4 a 5 Seren. Derbyniodd y cwmni Wobr Celfyddydau Hodge Foundation gan Gelfyddydau & Busnes Cymru yn 2024.

LINKTR.EE/GRANDAMBITION

  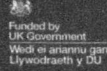
 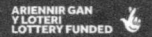

CAST

IZZI MCCORMACK JOHN *Kyla*

**Theatre includes / **Theatr yn cynnwys: *The Two Gentlemen of Verona* (Royal Shakespeare Company); *Love Steals Us From Loneliness* (Directed by Jake Harder). **Film and television includes / **Ffilm a theledu yn cynnwys: *Round These Parts* (CCNC Productions); short films / ffilmiau byr, *Salt, Shampoo, Fan Fiction* (BO15 Productions), *Best Before* (JLR Films).

LONDIWE MTHEMBU *Ruby*

**Theatre includes / **Theatr yn cynnwys: *Beauty and the Beast* (The Riverfront, Newport); *Much Ado About Nothing* (East London Shakespeare Festival); *Truth or Dare* (Theatr Clwyd); *An Inspector Calls, Macbeth* (Globe Players); *Children of Killers, Extremism* (Soho Theatre). **Film and television includes / **Ffilm a theledu yn cynnwys: *Galwad* (Sky / National Theatre Wales); short films / ffilmiau byr, *Growing Pains – The Feminist, The First Time*.

RICHARD ELIS *Cheney*

**For Sherman Theatre / **Ar gyfer Theatr y Sherman: *Cynnau Tân*. **Theatre includes / **Theatr yn cynnwys: *Beauty and the Beast, Robin Hood, Aladdin, Cinderella, Jack & the Beanstalk, Dick Whittington* (The Riverfront Newport); *Curtain Up, Measure for Measure, Two Princes, Hobson's Choice, Word for Word, Hard Times, Accidental Death of an Anarchist* (Theatr Clwyd); *The Lady from the Sea* (Theatr Cymru); *Beauty and the Beast, Robin Hood, Cinderella, Aladdin* (Hiss & Boo Company); *Bedroom Farce* (New Wolsey Theatre); *Dumb Show* (New Victoria Theatre); *Acqua Nero* (Sgript Cymru); *Peter Pan, Robin Hood, Murdered to Death* (UK Productions); *The Comedy of Errors* (Stafford Gatehouse Theatre); *Cinderella* (Hackney Empire); *Small Change* (Basingstoke).

RACHEL REDFORD *Sadie*

**For Sherman Theatre / **Ar gyfer Theatr y Sherman: *It's A Family Affair (We'll Settle It Ourselves)*. **Theatre includes / **Theatr yn cynnwys: *A Russian Doll* (Barn Theatre); *The Jungle* (The Young Vic / Playhouse Theatre / St. Ann's Warehouse, New York / The Curran,

San Francisco); *The Crucible* (Manchester Royal Exchange); *Luna Gale* (Hampstead Theatre); *Closer* (Donmar Warehouse); *A Ghost from a Perfect Place* (The Arcola); *Adler and Gibb* (Royal Court Theatre); *Not the Worst Place* (Paines Plough); *Parallel Lines* (Chapter Arts Centre / Dirty Protest); *Romeo & Juliet* (Black Rat Productions). **Film and television includes /** Ffilm a theledu yn cynnwys: *The Return of the Yuletide Kid* (BBC); *Testament of Youth* (Heyday Films); *The Riot Club* (Blueprint Pictures); *Nights* (short film / ffilm fer) (RADA); *Shadow and Bone* (Netflix); *House of the Dragon* (HBO); *Gap Year* (Eleven Films Ltd).

CREATIVE TEAM / TÎM CREADIGOL

REBECCA JADE HAMMOND Writer / *Ysgrifennwr*

For Sherman Theatre / Ar gyfer Theatr y Sherman: *Mad Margot* (& RWCMD / The Yard), *Lung Water,* (online / ar-lein & National Theatre Wales / Chippy Lane Productions). **Theatre writing includes /** Ysgrifennu Theatr yn cynnwys: *Right Where We Left Us* (Chapter, Cardiff / Chippy Lane Productions Ltd); *Welcome To Bettyland* (LAMDA). She is currently under commission with Theatr Clwyd writing a new historical play about Margaret Beaufort and developing a new Welsh musical *Toy Mic Trev* with her company Chippy Lane Productions Ltd. **Television writing includes /** Ysgrifennu Teledu yn cynnwys: she is writing a new comedy-drama for television called *Full Out* about cheerleading with co-writer Tanya Reynolds. Rebecca is Artistic Director of Chippy Lane Productions Ltd. She teaches acting for screen at LAMDA, RWCMD and Italia Conti. She is a member of Faber Academy, writing her first fiction novel, *Limerence*, and recently joined BBC Voices on their writing for television programme. Rebecca yw Cyfarwyddwr Artistig Chippy Lane Productions Ltd. Mae'n dysgu actio i'r sgrin yn LAMDA, CBCDC ac Italia Conti. Mae hi'n aelod o Academi Faber, yn ysgrifennu ei nofel ffuglen gyntaf, *Limerence*, ac yn ddiweddar wedi ymuno â BBC Voices ar eu gwaith ysgrifennu i raglen deledu.

HANNAH NOONE Director / *Cyfarwyddwr*

For Sherman Theatre / Ar gyfer Theatr y Sherman: *The Wife of Cyncoed, Ten / Deg, Lung Water, (online / ar-lein* & National Theatre Wales / Chippy Lane Productions), *Between Eternity & Time* (& RWCMD). **Theatre includes /** Theatr yn cynnwys: *Cinderella, The Snow Queen* (Storyhouse); *Truth* (Theatr Clwyd); Offie-nominated *The Elixir of Love* (King's Head Theatre); *The In-between, Y Teimlad / That Feeling* (National Youth Theatre of Wales / Theatr Clwyd); *Nightmare Scenario* (Opera Sonic); *Worlds Apart in War* (Theatr Clwyd / National Trust); *A Soldier's Tale* (Edinburgh Incidental Orchestra); *BoHo* (Theatr Clwyd / Hijinx); *Sweet Charity, The Welkin, Wife, London Road, Arcadia*

(RWCMD). She was co-director to Tamara Harvey for the first UK National Tour of Olivier Award-winning *Home, I'm Darling* (NT / Clwyd / Bill Kenwright), and is an Associate Director of Chippy Lane Productions. She will make her directorial debut with Welsh National Opera this year with *Panig! Attack!!* to mark the 20th anniversary of WNO Youth Opera. / Roedd hi'n gyd-gyfarwyddwr i Tamara Harvey ar gyfer y daith genedlaethol gyntaf o'r ddrama ag enillodd wobr Olivier, *Home, I'm Darling* (NT / Clwyd / Bill Kenwright), ac mae'n Gyfarwyddwr Cyswllt Chippy Lane Productions. Bydd yn gwneud ei hymddangosiad cyntaf fel cyfarwyddwr gydag Opera Cenedlaethol Cymru eleni gyda *Panig! Attack!!* i nodi 20 mlynedd ers sefydlu Opera Ieuenctid WNO.

DENA DAVIES *Assistant Director*
Cyfarwyddwr Cynorthwyol

Dena Davies is a Swansea theatre-maker and a graduate of the Liverpool Institute for Performing Arts / Mae Dena Davies yn grewyr theatr o Abertawe ac wedi graddio o Liverpool Institute for Performing Arts. **Assistant Director credits include / Credydau Cyfarwyddwr Cynorthwyol yn cynnwys:** *Rapunzel* (Everyman Theatre); *MumFighter, Sorter* (Swansea Grand Theatre); *Rope* (Theatr Clwyd).

HANNAH WOLFE *Designer / Cynllunydd*

Theatre includes / Theatr yn cynnwys: *Gianni Schicci* (Copenhagen Opera Festival); *Il Pastore* (Buxton International Festival); *Last Easter* (The Orange Tree); *Where The Wild Things Are* (Shadwell Opera); *A Christmas Carol* (Theatre by the Lake); *Great Expectations, Frankenstein* (Southwark Playhouse); *The Wizard of Oz* (Pitlochry Festival Theatre); *Victoria's Knickers* (Soho Theatre); *Eugenius! The Musical* (The Other Palace); *The Cunning Little Vixen, The Lighthouse, In The Locked Room* (Royal College of Music); *Betrayal* (Salisbury Playhouse); *FOOD* (Finborough Theatre); *Robin Hood* (The Egg Theatre, Bath); *King Matt, Macbeth* (The Lyceum, Edinburgh); *Bullets Over Broadway, Lady Be Good, Bells Are Ringing* (Arts Educational Schools); *Hubbub* (Lakeside Arts, Nottingham); *The Innocent Mistress, London Road, The Gigantic Beard That Was Evil* (Bristol Old Vic Studio); *Love Steals Us From Loneliness* (Brewery Theatre, Bristol); *Kafka vs. Kafka* (Etcetera Theatre, London); *Amadis de Gaule* (Bloomsbury Theatre, London). **Film includes / Ffilm yn cynnwys:** *Serenade* and / a *Cherubino* (Tigerlily Films / Shadwell Opera for / ar gyfer Channel 4).

KATY MORISON *Lighting Designer / Cynllunydd Goleuo*

For Sherman Theatre / Ar gyfer Theatr y Sherman: *The Wife of Cyncoed, Elen Benfelen / Goldilocks, A Hero of the People, The Snow Queen,*

Woof, *Alice in Wonderland*, *Little Red Riding Hood / Yr Hugan Fach Goch*, *Corina Pavlova and the Lion's Roar*, *The Snow Tiger / Teigr yr Eira*. **Theatre includes /** Theatr yn cynnwys: *Cinderella* (Storyhouse, Chester); *The Suspicions of Mr Whicher* (Watermill); *Waldo's Circus of Magic & Terror* (Bristol Old Vic / UK Tour / Extraordinary Bodies); *A Gig for Ghosts* (Soho Upstairs / 45North); *A Dead Body in Taos*, *The Litten Trees* (Fuel Theatre); *The In-between* (National Youth Arts Wales / Theatr Clywd); *Anthem* (Wales Millennium Centre); *A Tale of Two Cities* (Lost Dog Dance); *Anfamol* (Theatr Cymru); *Typical Girls* (Clean Break / Sheffield Theatres); *Possible, Peggy's Song, For All I Care, Come Back Tomorrow, The Big Democracy Project* (National Theatre Wales); *Why Are People Clapping, Moving Is Everywhere, Forever* (National Dance Company Wales); *The Glee Club* (Stockroom); *American Nightmare, The Story, Hela, Seanmhair, Play/Silence, Sand, St Nicholas, Constellation Street, A Good Clean Heart* (The Other Room); *Exodus, The Good Earth* (Motherlode); *Crouch, Touch, Pause, Engage* (National Theatre Wales / Out of Joint); *Escape the Scaffold* (The Other Room / Theatre 503); *Sinners Club* (The Other Room / Gagglebabble / Theatr Clwyd).

TIC ASHFIELD *Sound Designer / Cynllunydd Sain*

For Sherman Theatre / Ar gyfer Theatr y Sherman: *Iphigenia yn Sblot*, *Housemates* (& Hijinx Theatre); *Heart of Cardiff*; *Lung Water* (online / ar-lein & National Theatre Wales / Sherman Theatre / Chippy Lane Productions); *Constellation Street* (online / ar-lein & National Theatre Wales / Sherman Theatre / The Other Room); *Ripples* (online / ar-lein & National Theatre Wales / RWCMD / CBCDC). **Theatre and Dance includes /** Theatr a Dawns yn cynnwys: *Kill Thy Neighbour* (Theatr Clwyd / Torch Theatre); *Meta vs Life* (Hijinx Theatre); *Es & Flo* (WMC / CMC / Kiln Theatre); *Pijin / Pigeon* (Theatr Cymru / Theatr Iolo); *Right Where We Left Us*, *Blue* (Chippy Lane Productions); *The Boy With Two Hearts* (WMC / CMC / National Theatre); *Anthem* (WMC / CMC); *Y Teimlad* (online – National Youth Arts Wales); *Rocket Launch Blaenavon* (Tin Shed Theatre); *Qwerin* (Osian Meilir); *Ghost Light* (Ffwrnes Theatre); *Are You O.K.?, Metamorphosis* (online / ar-lein – Hijinx Theatre); *Pryd Mae'r Haf?* (Theatr Cymru); *A Number, All But Gone, The Awkward Years, American Nightmare, The Story, Hela* (The Other Room); *The Gathering, {150}, The Tide Whisperer, For As Long As The Heart Beats, Storm III* (National Theatre Wales); *On Bear Ridge* (National Theatre Wales / The Royal Court); *Dear To Me | Annwyl i mi* (National Dance Company Wales); *The Invisible Woman* (Alisa Jenkins); *Peeling* (Taking Flight Theatre); *Cracked* (Emily Hinshelwood); *Bottom* (Willy Hudson); *Richard III, Henry VI, Romeo & Juliet* (Omidaze Productions); *Saturday Night Forever* (Joio), *Momentos of Leaving, Moment(o)s* (Elaine Paton); *Hard Times* (Lighthouse Theatre); *Cold Rolling* (Ballet Cymru); *My People* (Gwyn Emberton Dance); *Tir Sir Gar* (Theatr Cymru).

Hot Chicks

'Hope' is the thing with feathers –
That perches in the soul –
And sings the tune without the words –
And never stops – at all –

Emily Dickinson

Acknowledgements/Cydnabyddiaethau

Hannah Noone, John Donnelly, Papatango, Georgina Ruffhead, Rachel O'Riordan, Liz Daramola, Alex Hurst, Davina Moss, Rhys Warrington, Germma Orleans-Thompson

Actors
Gaby French, Sophie Melville, Lee Mengo, Rebecca Hayes, Stevie Raine, Foxy Hardman, Yasemin Özdemir, Charlotte O'Leary, Zadeiah Campbell-Davies, Celyn Cartwright, Elan Meirion, Gwyneth Keyworth, Isabella Colby Browne, Morgan Price-Evans, Rosie Sheehy, Lisa Diveney, Lola Jenkins, Kiera Watts, Richard Mylan, Michelle McTernan, Christian Patterson, Rachel Redford, Londiwe Mthembu, Izzi McCormack-John, Richard Elis

Project Support
The Peggy Ramsay Foundation, The Carne Trust, Philip Carne, The Lyric Hammersmith, The Haworth Agency, National Theatre Writing Group, Julia Barry, Joe Murphy, Sherman Theatre, Grand Ambition, Swansea Grand Theatre

Thank You/Diolch

So many have made this piece possible but I'd also love to highlight the following:

Firstly a massive thank you to Dom and the team at Methuen for their continued support in publishing me as a playwright. It is always incredible to be given this opportunity to be in print.

To my wonderful agent Georgina Ruffhead at The Haworth Agency. This piece led me to you and I am beyond grateful for your continued support and belief in my work.

To Grand Ambition, I cannot thank you enough for the belief in my work and for taking it into production. You lead with love and care for artists – your light is growing from Swansea and beyond. Also, to Sherman for their continued support of my work and for co-producing this important piece of theatre.

To CMET Swansea's Young Person's Panel, Y-HUB (YMCA Swansea) and SAFE Cardiff for their invaluable input and feedback, you've made my play better!

Thank you and I love you to Lucas (Lion) and Biscuit for always being there for me and keeping me safe and happy at what has been a difficult time in my life. To Mum and Abby, for their love and support over the years. We've survived and we keep going for Dad because he was everything.

Thank you to Beyoncé (Cowboy Carter) x

Lastly, Hannah Noone. One of my best friends, collaborators, chief-therapist and director extraordinaire. I couldn't have done this without you. I wouldn't have wanted to do it. I love you, thank you so much. WE FINALLY GOT SOMETHING OVER THE LINE!

Big Love/Cariad Mawr, RJH x

Hot Chicks

For/i Dad
You are and will always be everything.
Love you/Caru i ti x

Characters/Cymeriadau

Ruby, *female, 15*
Kyla, *female, 15*
Sadie, *female, 30s*
Cheney, *male, 50s*

Location/Lleoliad

A chicken shop in Penlan, Swansea, but it could also be in any seaside town across the UK.

Notes/Nodiadau

(/) indicates an interruption or cutoff in speech.

(. . .) indicates a search or trail off of thought.

(–) indicates immediate change of thought.

The grammar indicates delivery rather than being grammatically correct.

Music/Cerddoriaeth

I was listening to Welsh Hip Hop and R&B.

Scenes/Golygfeydd

The scene titles map a grooming cycle from the dramatist's research and observations.

Scene One	*Colliding/Cyd-Daro*
Scene Two	*Impressions/Argraffiadau*
Scene Three	*Peacocking/Swagro*
Scene Four	*Thriving/Llywyddo*
Scene Five	*Loyalty/Teyrngarwch*
Scene Six	*Claws/Crafangau*
Scene Seven	*Bite/Brathiad*
Scene Eight	*Chicks/Cywion*

Scene One

Colliding/*Cyd-Daro*

2024

A shop sits in the middle of a parade of shops, 'CHENEY'S CHICKEN'. The shop is tired, but as clean as a takeout joint could be.

Ruby *and* **Kyla** *enter watching TikTok videos on* **Kyla**'s *phone trying to recreate the dance.*

Cheney *sets down one box of chicken.*

Ruby   Where's tha chips?

Cheney   You got enough money?

Kyla   Yeah we do.

Ruby   We can't have chicken without chips.

Cheney   How much you got then?

Ruby   Like four quid.

Kyla   Actually, four quid twenty.

Cheney   You're still eighty pence short.

Kyla   Fuck sake.

Cheney   No f'ing!

Ruby   Oh, let us off will yer.

Cheney   Not today.

Kyla   Why?

Cheney   Because you girls are fleecing me.

Ruby   We'll give it back.

Kyla   Eventually.

Cheney   But you already owe me for yesterday.

Kyla Aw, I can't be bothered with you then.

Ruby Yeah don't bother.

Kyla They're dirty chips anyway.

Ruby Yeah smelly chips.

Cheney You'd inhale them if they were free.

Ruby Too right.

Cheney But they're not free are they?

Kyla Yer we go again.

Cheney Because nothing in /

Kyla/Ruby LIFE IS FUCKING FREE!

Cheney LIFE IS FREE!

Beat.

Exactly.

Kyla Yer so tight Chen.

Cheney Gotta be these days. You wouldn't ask yer dad for a free rad would you?

Kyla A rad?

Cheney A radiator.

Ruby Why would she need a free radiator?

Cheney You wouldn't ask him for free stuff all the time.

Kyla Couldn't give a shit about my dad.

Cheney You don't mean that.

Kyla Nan's changed the locks on him.

Cheney Has she?

Kyla I don't really want to talk about it so carry on counting yer chips.

Cheney Alright narky knickers.

Beat.

Ruby Do you want to talk about it with me?

Kyla No I don't.

Cheney *comes over with a can of pop.*

Cheney You're lucky I'm giving you one.

Kyla Tight as a camel's arse in a sandstorm you.

Ruby Always wanted to go on a camel to be fair.

Cheney *starts cleaning tables.*

Cheney You started revising girls?

Ruby Nope.

Cheney How come?

Kyla What's the point?

Cheney If you want to do something great you have to go to school.

Kyla Dun need it.

Cheney Everyone needs it.

Kyla You do alright? You're still alive.

Cheney Well I could have done better.

Kyla Once we get 100K followers we'll be making bank from brand deals and sponsors. Look at Mr Beast or Tana Mongeau, she made serious dollars in Vegas being pure white trash.

Ruby Yeah she's pure white viral trash.

Kyla Check you Rub that was sharp then.

Ruby And we need to go pure Swansea viral.

Kyla Don't overdo it, yeah. Anyway, it's just a matter of time.

Ruby Yeah, just a matter of time.

Kyla No need for school, we're schoolin life.

Ruby Schoolin life in Vegas.

Cheney *cackles to himself.*

Kyla What's so funny?

Cheney Vegas? How you pair gonna get to Vegas you ain't gotta pot to piss in?

Ruby Well, that's where yer wrong we've started a 'Vegas fund'.

Kyla Mmhmm.

Cheney Oh yeah and how much you got in there then?

Kyla None of yer beeswax.

Cheney Why on earth would you wanna go there?

Kyla Where the big money is.

Cheney I dunno if that's true.

Ruby They have pool parties every day.

Kyla Swanky casinos and celebrities just running wild.

Cheney Sounds like Magaluf back in the day.

Kyla Women get loads of free stuff.

Cheney You're not old enough to be in those casinos.

Kyla We're gonna earn serious bank then spunk the lot on shit.

Cheney Like those Kardashians.

Kyla Don't speak about those old basic bitches. More like James Charles when he dropped 100K on Amazon buying utter shit.

Ruby RIP.

Cheney Is he dead?

Kyla No, he was cancelled for 'accidentally snapping minors'.

Cheney Christ everyone's being cancelled.

Kyla 40.6 mill followers. Paedo.

Beat.

Ruby Total paedo, but he's got loads of money.

Cheney Money can't buy you happiness girls.

Kyla Na but it makes things easier.

Ruby And everyone looks happy on TikTok in Vegas.

Kyla Coz it's sick and we're gonna live out our dream in SIN CITY.

Beat.

Cheney What, the night club?

Kyla We wouldn't be seen dead there.

Ruby We mean the real Sin City.

Cheney They wouldn't let you in anyway.

Ruby We're gonna live the dream together and no one's gonna stop us.

Cheney You know why it's called Sin City dun you?

Kyla Dun care.

Cheney Gambling, drink, drugs, prostitution. Sin City is America's nickname for a place that was like hell. Why else d'u think it's in the desert?

8   Hot Chicks

Beat.

Ruby   Shit, We never knew that, did we Ky?

Sadie *enters on her phone.*

Kyla   Zero fucks given there.

They all look at **Sadie**.

Sadie   Do you have coffee to go?

Cheney's *flustered by her presence.*

Cheney   . . . Uh, yeah we do coffee.

Kyla   Get yer chin off the floor Chen.

Beat.

Cheney   Milk?

He's overwhelmed.

Sadie   Na, black.

Sadie's *gaze meets* **Kyla**'s.

Kyla   Oh, she's a real hot one in-she?

Sadie   I prefer classy but I'll take that as a compliment.

Kyla *walks to the counter parallel to* **Sadie** *waiting for coffee.*

Kyla   Anyway, as I was saying before I was *rudely* interrupted, how do you know all this about Vegas big-boy?

Cheney   Don't call me that, I'm old enough to be your father.

Ruby   Yer our sugar daddy in you.

Cheney *looks embarrassed at* **Sadie**.

Cheney   NO I'M NOT. THEY'RE YANKING MY CHAIN MADAM.

Kyla's *checking her phone.*

Ruby We're going together to Vegas aren't we Ky?

Kyla Course mush.

Cheney Oh my LOL.

Ruby What you LOL'ing at?

Cheney You pair dreaming of Vegas, it really tickled me that has.

Kyla Ew.

Ruby We ain't dreaming.

Kyla There's shit all happening around yer and it's freezing we're gonna go somewhere hot and do stuff.

Cheney And you think you can't do that yer?

Kyla I won't stop until we get there. We're gonna be Swansea's first TikTok stars in the U.S of A.

Ruby We are but, we don't wanna get cancelled.

Kyla We won't Rub, dun worry we ain't gonna be cancelled for faking cancer.

Cheney Who faked having cancer?

Sadie Brittany Miller.

Kyla She's TikTok infamous.

Cheney Oh yeah, her. I got you.

Kyla She got 50K when the sponsors thought she had cancer.

Sadie Embarrassing. She sold her fake trauma for/

Kyla She did but we don't want to sell our trauma. We have morals.

Ruby And standards.

Kyla And principles

Cheney Yeah yeah.

Ruby But I still watch her ...

Kyla/Ruby 'It's dinner time!'

Kyla 'Dishing up'.

Cheney The world's gone nuts.

Beat.

Kyla Anyway, that's our plan.

Cheney Sounds achievable.

Kyla OI DON'T GASLIGHT ME GARETH!

Sadie Sounds like a cracking plan.

Kyla Who asked you.

Cheney KYLA DUN BE RUDE!

Ruby Ky, you won't leave me yer will you?

Kyla Ain't got a choice, you're stuck to my arse.

Kyla *sits back down next to* **Ruby** *and opens a can of pop.*

Ruby Seriously though Ky, how are we gonna pay for Vegas?

Beat.

Kyla Might get a job yer?

Cheney Dream on!

Kyla Na, I'm too highbrow for this joint.

Ruby *spots a bracelet on the floor by the entrance and picks it up.*

Ruby Chen, there's a bracelet on the floor.

Sadie *checks her wrist and realises it's hers.*

Sadie Shit that's mine.

Kyla Uh, how do we know it's yours?

Ruby Because she just said Ky.

Kyla You could be just saying it is.

Cheney Give it back to the lovely woman now.

Sadie . . . It's fine.

Cheney It's not.

Sadie How do I prove to you it's mine?

Kyla . . . I dunno.

Beat.

. . . What brand is it?

Sadie Tiffany.

Kyla A bit obvious everyone knows Tiffany.

Sadie Tiffany owner are you?

Kyla Nope, not yet.

Sadie So, you could be trying to keep it for yourself then.

Pause.

My name's on the back. Sadie.

Kyla . . . Sure about that?

Ruby Ky that's her name, give it back.

She tosses it back to her.

It looks pricey.

Sadie It wasn't that much.

Kyla I think Tiffany's a bit . . .

Sadie What?

Kyla Overrated.

Ruby Can I try it on?

Sadie   Go ahead.

Ruby *takes the bracelet.*

Kyla   Your boyfriend must really like you.

Sadie   Don't have one. I bought this for myself.

Ruby   D'u earn lots of money then?

Cheney   Ruby!

Sadie   No, it's OK. I've got my own business.

Ruby   WOAH! That's amazing.

Kyla's *on her phone looking at TikTok.*

Sadie   It's hard work though.

Sadie's *phone pings.*

I need to go.

Ruby *hands back the bracelet.*

Sadie   You can keep it if you want.

Beat.

Ruby   . . . What?

Sadie   I've got like three others.

Kyla *looks up from her phone.*

Ruby   Oh I couldn't.

She hands it to her.

Sadie   I don't want anything for it.

Ruby   It's OK.

Sadie   Well then let me get yer tea then.

She hands **Cheney** *a twenty pound note.*

Sadie   Whatever they want, it's on me.

Cheney Don't feel you should, they're always here sponging off me.

Kyla We don't sponge!

Ruby We do . . . a bit.

Sadie Just get me tea next time.

Ruby When will that be?

Sadie Soon I imagine. I've got a weakness for chicken.

Sadie *rushes out the door.*

Ruby, **Kyla** *and* **Cheney** *look on after her.*

Ruby She is . . . something else.

Cheney . . . She is.

Both **Kyla** *and* **Ruby** *laugh and celebrate.*

Ruby One of everything Chen!

Kyla And hurry the fuck up.

Cheney *rolls his eyes and starts to put chicken in the fryer.*

Scene Two

Impressions/*Argraffiadau*

A week later.

Cheney *stocks shelves behind the counter.*

Ruby *and* **Kyla** *are lying on a table,* **Kyla** *has her feet in the air.*

Ruby They look incredible.

Kyla Do you think the toe rings are overkill?

Ruby Na, just enough.

Kyla Gotta give my public what they want.

Ruby How many you got on your OnlyFans?

Kyla Thirty-nine.

Ruby Who'd have thought that many people love feet that much to pay for it.

Kyla People will wank over any old things these days. My nan said her supervisor at work has started selling her farts in jars for twenty quid a pop.

Ruby That's rank.

Kyla I know but money's money and imagine having that much you wouldn't need to worry about a thing.

Ruby I dunno what I'd do with all that money?

Kyla I'd drape myself in Balenciaga and drop some serious dollars in Vegas.

Sadie *enters*.

Ruby Sadie! We were wondering when we'd see you again?

Sadie This place is lush. I had to come back.

Kyla Really? It's like a shit disco with all the lights flashing outside.

Cheney It's to attract attention.

Kyla Yeah the wrong kind.

Sadie I feel like I've stumbled across something special.

Cheney *sets down three boxes of chicken*.

Cheney It pulls you in.

Sadie And obviously great chicken.

Cheney I do make it good.

Sadie I'll need your secret.

Cheney You can have it . . . but it will come at a price.

Beat.

Scene Two

Ruby Are you flirting?

Cheney I'm a professional.

Kyla Oh zip it Chen.

Cheney I'll zip you in a minute.

Sadie *looks at her phone.*

Sadie Aw shit.

Kyla Who's all the chicken for?

Sadie They've stood me up.

Cheney Oh no and you were so sweet to phone ahead with the order /

Ruby We can take it off your hands.

Kyla Who's all the chicken for?

Sadie I was meeting someone but they stood me up.

Ruby We can take it off your hands.

Cheney Oh yer comes the dust bin. Or what do they say in America . . . TRASH CAN?

Ruby I'm not a trash can.

Sadie Go ahead.

Kyla We don't want it.

Sadie She looks hungry?

Kyla Ruby needs to watch her figure.

Ruby I don't.

Kyla She wasn't born with a fast metabolism.

Sadie You've got good genes Kayla.

Kyla Kyla.

Sadie Oh really? It's so similar.

Ruby Look at my cankles Sadie.

She shows **Sadie** *her ankles.*

Sadie How old are you?

Ruby We're nearly sixteen.

Sadie You look older.

Ruby Thanks.

Sadie Don't worry about your ankles, your body will grow into them.

Kyla I want a body like a Coke bottle.

Ruby Where's your coat from?

Sadie Gucci.

Kyla Gucci's on its way up again in-it?

Sadie Wouldn't be wearing it if it wasn't.

Sadie's *phone rings.*

Ruby Can I try it on?

She chucks the coat at **Ruby** *then goes outside to take the call.*

Kyla She's trying too hard her.

Ruby I think she's stuns.

Kyla She's generic.

Cheney I think she's a nice woman.

Kyla We didn't ask you.

Ruby *struts.*

Cheney Is Sadie stepping on your patch Ky?

Kyla *clicks her fingers.*

Kyla Go get us Diet Coke now! Chop chop.

Ruby Choppity chop.

Scene Two   17

Cheney   One of these days I will snap.

Kyla   Yeah yeah.

Cheney   I will, I will snap.

Kyla   Go and snap at the pickled eggs then.

Cheney *exits.*

Kyla   She's odd she is.

Ruby   I don't care what you say I like her.

Kyla   She doesn't look like she eats chicken.

Ruby   A girl's gotta eat. She's got good genes like you . . . You look like her?

Kyla   No I don't.

Ruby   You do . . . you could be sisters.

Kyla   Jog on!

Ruby *and* **Kyla** *cackle.*

Sadie *walks back in.*

Sadie   Christ.

Kyla   What's the face for?

Sadie   Just busy and sometimes if you want a job done well you gotta do it yourself.

Ruby   Do you have loads of people working for you?

Sadie   A few.

Ruby   Wow.

Sadie   You ain't got a tampon on you . . . Ruby is it?

Ruby   Yeah.

Ruby *goes into her bag.*

Kyla   No you don't. She's a late bloomer.

Kyla *goes into her bag and pulls out a tampon.*

Sadie Have you not started yet?

Ruby *looks embarrassed.*

Kyla You wouldn't think it would you Sadez.

Ruby Ky!

Sadie All the best girls start late anyway.

Sadie *takes the tampon from* **Kyla**.

Ruby You reckon?

Sadie I didn't start until I was seventeen.

Ruby Didn't you?

Sadie It comes when it comes.

Ruby That makes me feel a whole lot better.

Kyla Kiss arse.

Sadie One day something will happen and you'll just bleed.

Beat.

Kyla TMI.

Sadie *laughs and goes to the toilet.*

Kyla She better give me some coin for that tampon.

Ruby *rubs her belly.*

Kyla . . . Why are you looking like that?

Ruby Like what?

Kyla Like you need a big dump because I always know when that is.

Ruby That's just my face.

Kyla's *phone pings, she looks at it then smiles.*

Ruby Is it Eli?

Kyla . . . Yeah.

Cheney *enters from out the back.*

Ruby He's so in love with you Ky.

Cheney They always are in the beginning.

Kyla What happened to our Diet Cokes?

Cheney We're out.

Kyla This place is shit.

Ruby So shit.

Cheney Stop coming yer then.

Kyla Let's ignore him.

She shows it to **Ruby**.

Ruby Oh . . . my . . . god.

Kyla . . . Yeah.

Ruby It's so /

Kyla Big?

Ruby No, it's scary.

Kyla It's not.

Ruby It hasn't got the . . .

Kyla What?

Ruby You know the . . .

Kyla What?

Ruby The . . . um, you know like . . . the bit on the top.

Kyla Circumcised in-he.

Ruby Why?

Kyla Religion and stuff.

Ruby Aw, is Eli religious?

Kyla His family are.

Ruby Wow, people do that?

Kyla What?

Ruby Like religion and stuff.

Kyla Well, Dad found god when he was sectioned.

Ruby So, is yer dad?

Kyla What?

Ruby You know, got the top bit on the /

Kyla EW, I DUNNO.

Ruby Soz.

Kyla I'm surprised you noticed considering you've never seen one.

Ruby I have seen one.

Kyla When?

Ruby Last year.

Kyla Biology doesn't count.

Ruby I've not just seen one in biology.

Kyla Where else have you seen one then?

Beat.

Ruby Porn.

Kyla Porn?

Cheney Porn?!

Ruby Yeah porn.

Sadie *enters from the toilet moisturising her hands.*

Scene Two 21

Cheney You pair shouldn't be watching that stuff.

Ruby Do you watch porn Chen?

Cheney I'm not answering that.

Kyla Because you obviously do.

Cheney I don't need it. I got ladies lining up for me outside the shop.

Kyla What like Ruby's Aunty Cora. Have you seen the state of her?

Ruby She's had a hard life Ky.

Kyla She likes it hard from what I yer.

Cheney Where'd you get that from?

Kyla How can someone look so much like a warthog?

Sadie Poor Aunty Cora.

Ruby Yeah poor Aunty Cora.

Kyla Are you attracted to animals Chen? There's a name for that isn't there.

Cheney She doesn't look like a warthog.

Kyla What's it called again?

Cheney And I am not attracted to animals. I mean I like them, but not like that /

Sadie Beastiality! But I'm sure he's not into that.

Ruby Are you into animals Chen and uh-beastiality?

Kyla Just women who look like warthogs.

Ruby You like women who look like animals Chen?

Kyla That's weird.

Ruby Yeah, well weird.

Cheney That'll do girls.

Kyla Stop listening in then.

Cheney Well stop speaking so loudly then!

Cheney *leaves.*

Sadie Why are you watching porn?

Ruby Holly said it's good to do research in prep for the real thing.

Kyla Holly said?

Ruby Yeah.

Kyla I'm not being funny bu Holly's a fridge. Like she's had any boys with that breath. I'm glad we binned her off.

Ruby Yeah me too . . .

Kyla Fuck her! We're a duo and we're stuns.

Sadie You are both stuns.

Kyla If they wanna revise then let em carry on.

Sadie Don't be a sheep.

Kyla Exactly what I always say. Ruby wants to go to college, like behave.

Kyla *cackles.*

Ruby I wanna learn music.

Kyla Music? You'd be shit at music.

Sadie I bet you've got a lovely voice.

Ruby I do. Kyla's just jelly because she sounds like a cat being strangled.

Kyla Whatever, you're hardly gonna be Sabrina Carpenter.

Sadie Sing for me.

Ruby No.

Sadie Go on.

Ruby I couldn't.

Sadie Do it.

She bursts suddenly into song.

Kyla That's enough!

Ruby Whatever.

Ruby *starts to twirl in* **Sadie**'s *Gucci coat.*

Ruby I love this coat, Sadie.

Kyla How much was it?

Sadie More than a Primark special.

Ruby Everything I'm wearing is from Primarni.

Sadie Which is great, but every lady wants a bit of designer.

Kyla It's not my style to be honest.

Ruby I think it's fabulous.

Kyla It's a bit OTT, take it off.

Ruby It's fab-you-lous Kyla and you know it! Salty.

Kyla I'm not salty.

Sadie I think she might be . . . a bit salty.

Ruby *returns* **Sadie**'s *coat reluctantly and starts licking the chicken box.*

Kyla And can you stop eating like that, it's going through me yer minger.

Beat.

Ruby There's nothing in the house.

Kyla He's useless, your Dad.

Sadie All Dads are useless.

Ruby I had to eat a jar of pickled onions last night. Got the shits.

Kyla Holy shit!

Ruby There was a lot of shit but there was nothing holy about it.

They all laugh.

Kyla D'u work then?

Sadie I told you I have my own business.

Kyla Doing wha?

Sadie A bit of everything.

Kyla Like wha?

Sadie I've always been entrepreneurial.

Ruby Entre-wha?

Sadie Someone driven to be super successful.

Ruby Like a girl boss.

Sadie Yeah, I guess.

Kyla What type of business you in?

Sadie Delivery services.

Ruby Like Deliveroo?

Sadie Yeah . . . a bit.

Kyla Delivering wha?

Sadie I gotta say you look incredible in my coat.

Ruby Really? I wish it was mine.

Sadie Well sadly I can't give you that but I do have a bag of stuff I don't wear anymore you can have that?

Ruby For free?

Beat.

Sadie Tell you what, put your numbers in my phone.

Ruby Oh. My. God. Yes! We can start a group chat.

Kyla Oh christ, Ruby's obsessed with starting group chats.

Ruby Yes! What shall we call ourselves?

Ruby *takes* **Sadie**'s *phone and starts creating a group chat.*

Sadie Whatever you want.

Pause.

Ruby Hot Chicks!

Kyla Don't be fucking stupid.

Ruby Don't call me stupid.

Sadie I love it.

Kyla Really?

Sadie Yeah.

Kyla It'd just not be very original like.

Ruby Well, it's two against one.

Sadie Have you put your numbers in my phone?

Kyla I haven't given my consent.

Ruby *gives the phone back to* **Sadie**.

Ruby Give over Ky we're a trio of hot chicks.

Sadie That we are.

Kyla Christ.

Ruby We're chicks, who eat chicks and we're hot. Selfie for the group!

Ruby *makes* **Sadie** *and* **Kyla** *crowd together to take a selfie.*

Ruby Say . . . hot chicks?!

All   . . . HOT CHICKS!

The picture is taken and assigned to their group chat.

Sadie *has a flurry of pings on her phone and she looks at it.*

Sadie   Shit I'm so busy at the moment.

Pause.

Kyla   We could help you . . . if the price is right.

Sadie   That's sweet but I don't think so.

Kyla   We're not sixteen you wouldn't have to put us on the books.

Beat.

Sadie   Well, it's all going on up there in-it?

Her phone pings and pings.

I'll message you later girls.

She leaves.

Kyla   Wanted to test her and see if she'd pay us.

Ruby   Backfired on your arse then.

Kyla   I ain't doing nothing for free.

Ruby   She didn't give you a job though did she?

Kyla   And that's her loss.

Cheney *comes out with some cans of fruit pop and sets them down.*

Kyla   I'm not drinking that it's rank.

Cheney   Well beggars can't be choosers.

Ruby   It's got fruit in it.

Kyla   And?

Ruby   One of your five a day.

Ruby *starts strutting up and down the shop.*

Ruby Have I got it?

Kyla What?

Ruby Her walk.

Kyla Whose?

Ruby Sadie's.

Kyla You worry me you do.

Cheney No wait. Hang on . . . do it again?

Ruby *struts.*

Ruby So?

Cheney Yeah.

Ruby Have I?

Cheney What?

Ruby Got Sadie's walk?

Pause.

Cheney . . . Nowhere near.

Cheney *leaves to prep food out the back.*

Their phones ping.

Ruby Sadie's messaged! She thinks she may have left a rucksack.

Kyla She doesn't look like the type to have a rucksack.

Ruby Did you see her nails? They looked like they cost serious money.

Kyla Serious money.

Their phones ping.

Ruby Can you help me look for it Ky?

Their phones ping.

Kyla   What did yer last slave die of?

Ruby   She said she'll give us money if we drop it off.

Kyla   I'll help.

Kyla *begins to look.*

Where do we need to drop it?

Beat.

Ruby   Sketty.

Kyla   Sketty?! Fancy as fuck over there.

Ruby   I don't wanna go over there Ky it's already dark.

Kyla   Don't be such a baby.

Ruby   Bu /

Kyla   Does she live in Sketty?

Ruby   She needs us to drop off the bag.

Kyla *stops looking.*

Kyla   It's probably drugs.

Ruby   Drugs?

Kyla   What else would it be?

Beat.

Ruby   I don't wanna do drugs Ky.

Kyla   Yer not doing them you're running them.

Kyla *goes to the toilet to look for the bag.*

Ruby   I don't want to get involved with all that.

Kyla *calls out from the toilet.*

Kyla   Found it!

Ruby   Maybe we should keep hold of it until we see Sadie.

Kyla She's paying so what we got to lose?

Ruby Ky!

Kyla *sends a message to the group chat.*

Their phones ping.

Kyla She said she owes us big time . . . Right, let's go.

Ruby Should we look inside it and /

Kyla No, we don't look inside it's not our business to.

Ruby But it might be a bomb or something.

Kyla Do you wanna get to Vegas or not?

Cheney *comes in from out back.*

Cheney I found two dusty Diets they say 2019 bu no one really pays any attention to that stuff anymore.

Kyla We're going.

Ruby Soz Chen.

Cheney But Ruby, you said you'd help with the stock take for a Peter's Pie?

Ruby I can't I got stuff to do.

Kyla And she's shit at maths anyway.

They both exit, **Cheney** *looks on after them.*

Scene Three

Peacocking/*Swagro*

A week later.

Cheney *is on his knees clearing up a mess of chips on the floor as the girls walk in.*

Ruby Chen, can I get that chicken you fried the other week.

Beat.

Cheney Do I look like I'm serving?

Ruby You know the one you fried in cherry pop.

She goes to walk behind the counter.

Cheney DON'T YOU DARE GO BEHIND THERE!

Pause.

Kyla WOAH!

Ruby No need to get all you know 'The Hulk' on us.

Kyla You did go a bit green then.

Ruby Like properly angry.

Cheney I need to have boundaries.

Kyla What the fuck you on?

Cheney There's clear boundaries between you and the counter. I don't want you going behind there.

Ruby Sorry Chen.

Pause.

Cheney . . . Aw, go on-en then I'll make some.

Ruby Yes!

He goes behind the counter.

Cheney I'll put some cayenne in to give it a kick. Maybe some panko breadcrumbs.

Ruby I'll sweep the floor for you.

Ruby *starts sweeping up for* **Cheney**.

Kyla You need to call the police on those kids Chen. They bricked the windows in the pub the other night. Bloody asbos.

Cheney Like you know what an asbo is.

Scene Three 31

Kyla I do mush my mam and dad were king and queen of them.

Cheney The police say I'm making this place a target after I got robbed yer in the summer. They think I should shut up shop and leave but I can't do it.

Kyla Don't you wanna leave Swansea?

Cheney Same shit different city.

Ruby 'Pretty shitty city.'

Cheney It's our city dun you forget it.

Kyla But it's dead round yer, everything's dying.

Cheney Can't be that bad if Sadie's around.

Kyla Yeah, she's successful.

Cheney 'You gotta go there to come back.'

Kyla Exactly.

Cheney Stereophonics?

Kyla Who?

Cheney Never mind. It used to be buzzing around here. Mam used to make me peel double potatoes for chips. All the chicken we went through. She used to joke that we should get a coop out the back and cut out the middleman.

Kyla Dad said it attracted too many dodgy types.

Cheney Well he would know.

Beat.

Kyla What's that s'pose to mean?

Cheney Just he was yer all the time with his mates on their bikes and . . .

Kyla Wha?

Cheney Yer dad had the pick of the girls he was a bit of a player. I always wanted a bit of what he had.

Kyla I bet they wouldn't look twice at him now. He's barely got any teeth from being kicked in the other week.

Ruby I thought he super glued them back in.

Kyla He did.

Cheney Well he was a looker back then.

Kyla He stole Nan's wedding ring the other week and it turns out the diamond was plastic. Me and Nan pissed ourselves. Thick cunt.

Sadie *enters with a big bag of clothes.*

Sadie Gifts for my chicks.

Kyla KILLER!

They start digging through the clothes.

Ruby Oh my god this is so sparkly.

Kyla You and sparkles. Is this real?

Sadie Three seasons old but yeah.

Kyla Class.

Ruby *tries on a jacket.*

Ruby Are you sure we can have all this Sadie?

Sadie I don't want it.

Ruby I feel a million dollars in this thing.

Sadie You look it.

Ruby I've just copied you.

Kyla Yeah copycat.

Sadie Greatest form of flattery, imitation.

Kyla *goes into the toilet to try on an outfit.*

Ruby I used to try and copy what Jilly did all the time.

Sadie Jilly?

Ruby Oh that's what Ky told me to call her, she's no longer my mam.

Sadie Where is she?

Ruby I dunno where she went.

Sadie Oh yeah, my mum did that.

Ruby Did she?

Sadie It happens. Some women aren't meant to be mums.

Ruby Do you not miss her though, yer mam?

Sadie It sounds silly . . . but I used to pray she'd come back to save me one day.

Ruby . . . I do that.

Sadie But then I grew out of it.

Ruby Yeah . . . I need to do that.

Sadie You can do whatever you want to do if you put yourself out there. Scare yourself. I came from nothing, everything was against me but . . . I've made the best of it.

Cheney *bangs on the toilet door.*

Cheney Hurry up Ky I need to clean in there.

Kyla Don't fucking rush me.

Cheney Cut the f'ing will you. It's a family joint not your bedroom.

Kyla When was the last time you had a family in Chen?

Cheney . . . Uh /

Kyla *struts out the toilets in her new threads.*

Kyla Better take that family meal off the menu then, it's a ruse.

Ruby Oh my god you look . . .

Cheney Ridiculous. No offence Sadie.

Sadie None taken.

Cheney It's a no from me.

Kyla What do you know about fashion Tommy Tabard?

Cheney I may be Tommy Tabard, but at least my tabard fits.

Sadie Can I get a cup of coffee?

Cheney Black?

Sadie So efficient.

Cheney Thank you.

Kyla She's not interested in middle aged men Chen.

Sadie Ah, middle aged men bring experience to the table.

Cheney You hear that Kyla? Listen to this woman, she knows what's what. You could learn a thing or two from her girls.

Cheney *leaves.*

Sadie Boys will love you looking like that.

Ruby D'u reckon?

Sadie Do up a couple of the buttons, give 'em a bit of mystery.

Ruby We look just like you now.

Sadie You look better.

Kyla Yer bullshitting us there.

Sadie Does this face look like bullshit?

Ruby No it's an honest face.

Kyla Oh I dunno about tha. Did your mate get the bag OK?

Sadie Yeah, my god I would have been in some much shit for leaving it. I owe you big style for that.

Kyla Dun mention it we got your back.

Sadie *goes into her pocket to bring some money out.*

Ruby Oh, we don't need anything.

Sadie But, you did work for me.

She pulls out two envelopes of money and hands it to them.

Ruby We can't take this.

Sadie You can.

Kyla She's right, we can.

Sadie You can buy proper Jordans rather than those fake ones you got on.

Ruby But we /

Cheney *walks back with the coffee.*

Sadie Put it away.

Ruby All we did was post something we don't /

Sadie Just put it away!

Cheney *walks over.*

Ruby *hides the money under the clothes and* **Kyla** *puts hers in her jacket.*

Cheney Coffee my queen.

Beat.

Sadie Can I get it in a takeaway cup?

Cheney Of course. For you, anything.

Kyla She's not interested.

Sadie I might be.

Her and **Cheney** *exchange a smile and he prances out the back.*

Kyla You're not really are you? Old Chen?

Sadie The older the better.

Kyla Why?

Sadie Because you can wrap them around your little finger.

Kyla I don't want to be old and wrinkly.

Sadie Don't be ageist now.

Kyla Just stating facts, I'm gonna get shitloads of botox before I let the wrinkles come for me.

Sadie It's a lot of money to keep that up.

Kyla Well I'll be shitting twenties by that point.

Sadie Oh yeah, how are you gonna get enough twenties to shit then?

Kyla Well I was thinking we were thinking we could help with your deliveries.

Ruby Were we?

Kyla Yeah.

Sadie Well, that's convenient.

Kyla So we'd like to help you with your deliveries.

Sadie You mean drop offs?

Kyla . . . Yeah, drop offs.

Sadie It's a lot of responsibility.

Kyla We posted stuff before.

Sadie That was a one off.

Scene Three

Kyla We did you a favour.

Sadie That's not how it works.

Kyla You said you owe us.

Sadie I've paid you.

Kyla But we wanna make money don't we Rub. No need to go through the books.

Sadie Thank you for being so keen but I don't need anyone to /

Kyla We know it's drugs.

Cheney *comes in with a takeaway cup.*

Cheney Coffee to go for mademoiselle.

Sadie Start me a tab.

He goes back to restocking cans.

Kyla We've got a 100 per cent track record.

Sadie On one drop off.

Kyla Put us on probation then.

Her phone pings.

Sadie I'll think about it.

She answers the phone and leaves.

Cheney *puts on one of the jackets.*

Kyla You look like a bloated Christmas bauble.

Cheney *comes across an envelope of money.*

Cheney What's all this?

Kyla *snatches it back.*

Kyla None of yer business.

Cheney Where'd you get all that?

Kyla Nowhere.

Cheney Ruby?

Ruby . . .

Kyla It's guilt money from Dad.

Their phones ping.

Cheney Don't take his money Ky.

Kyla I'll do what I like.

Cheney Money always comes with strings.

Kyla He's a shit dad so I'm just gonna fleece him for cash.

Cheney Be careful is all I'm saying.

Cheney *walks back behind the counter.*

Kyla She's messaged she's gonna give us a shot.

Ruby I dunno if I wanna do this Ky.

Kyla Why not?

Ruby . . .

Kyla What's the worst that can happen?

Ruby Nothing bu /

Kyla We literally have nothing to lose. You don't need to be scared. I always got your back and we'll be in Vegas by the summer.

Beat.

Ruby D'u reckon?

Kyla No fucking doubt mush.

The following action happens over three months and should feel like a series of TikTok videos being made by the girls and **Sadie**. *Showing their evolving wardrobe hauls, buying sprees, rucksacks of food, money, chicken, chicken, chicken.*

Scene Four

Thriving/*Llywyddo*

Three months later.

Sadie *is covering up a bruise on* **Kyla**'s *cheek.*

Kyla Aww fuck! I could have floored him given half a chance. I'm tamping, raging like /

Sadie I've sorted it.

Kyla You sure?

Sadie You could never tell. You've both gotten so good it's like you've been doing it for years.

Kyla He just came at me.

Sadie Sometimes that happens but yer fast and the main thing is you managed to keep hold of the cash and look after yourself.

Kyla I'd have taken him down no messing.

Sadie I know you can handle yourself that's why I sent you and not Ruby. Did yer nan notice?

Kyla She wouldn't care if I walked out the house naked with a vajazzle.

Sadie Do you not get on?

Kyla Na we do like bu she works all the time so she's never there.

Sadie . . . That's a lot.

Kyla I can look after myself. I'm not like Ruby she needs looking after and her dad's a twat so I'm her guardian these days.

Sadie That's really decent of you. You look great by the way.

Kyla Nothing beats walking down the road feeling a million dollars.

Sadie Nothing beats strutting down the strip in Vegas feeling a billion.

Kyla Yeah, we're a bit far off from Vegas . . . I need to stop spending.

Sadie I've got a deal coming with an epic payout don't worry.

Kyla Are you sure you dun want anything for all this?

Sadie It's OK I get loads of it for free.

Kyla But this is like five hundred quids worth.

Sadie It's fine you can have it.

Kyla Nice. I dun know anyone around yer who'd spend fifty quid on eyeliner.

Sadie Yeah but look at the difference. When you've got good products on your skin you instantly feel better.

Kyla *goes to take a selfie.*

Kyla Yeah I agree bu, Dad says I look like a twat.

Sadie What do dads know? Nothing.

Kyla Yeah they're useless.

Sadie And controlling. When I left I vowed I would control my own life and my own money.

Kyla Yer so right.

Sadie As he always says, I'm a lone wolf.

Kyla Yeah bu, don't you wan a boyfriend?

Sadie If I want one I get one.

Kyla You're lucky you can pick and choose.

Sadie You've got Eli though, how's that going?

Scene Four

Kyla He just wants to play on his XBox all the time.

Sadie Are you not having good sex then?

Kyla Yeah . . . course I am what you take me for.

Kyla *looks a bit embarrassed.*

Sadie You know what you need? An older man. They'll give you the experiences you're missing out on.

Kyla I quite like Eli really I dun need /

Sadie Let me have a think about who I could set you up with.

Kyla I was thinking of moving on anyway.

Sadie How come Ruby doesn't have a boyfriend?

Kyla I think she's scared of boys.

Sadie We need to help her. Where is she?

Kyla She's upset I got hit and has been crying wanting her mam.

Sadie Do you cry for your mum?

Kyla Never had one.

Sadie Well you came out of someone.

Kyla I can't believe I came out of her like, bu – What I mean is, any woman can give birth but not everyone can be a mam.

Sadie That's smart . . .

Kyla I know.

Sadie You could do anything you know that?

Kyla Teachers say that to me, they say I hide it.

Sadie You hide it?

Kyla Yeah behind attitude and authority issues.

Sadie I hadn't noticed that.

Kyla I should be in the top set but they keep me in the bottom. Even though I read *The Handmaid's Tale* in two hours when Holly was only on chapter one. I'd never agree to being a baby machine.

Sadie What's Ruby like at school?

Kyla She's a bit /

Sadie Stupid.

Kyla She's not . . . she's just. She finds it hard to focus like.

Sadie I get you, fuck school.

Kyla Yeah fuck school.

Sadie They don't deserve you and Ruby.

Kyla They don't.

Sadie Is Ruby not coming today?

Kyla . . . Why'd you wan her yer?

Sadie Tell her to come meet us. Tell her if she doesn't come I'll take all my clothes back.

Kyla Oh she won't want that. She'll run faster than her cankles can carry her.

Kyla *begins typing a message.*

Their phones ping.

She thinks you're mad at her.

Sadie Let's blank her when she comes in.

Cheney Do you girls want anything?

Sadie Three Diet Cokes please Chen.

Cheney Coming up.

He leaves to go out the back.

Sadie Fascinating person Chen.

Kyla My dad said he was slow in school.

Sadie He's outsmarted them all now.

Kyla It was his mum's business; he's hardly Elon Musk.

Sadie Still he's keeping it going.

Kyla But everything in yers knackered.

Sadie Everything is worn out, yeah, but it's clean as a whistle.

Kyla Chen's OCD and obsessed with bleach.

Sadie He's got pride in his work.

Kyla I think he's anal as to be honest. It's too clean.

Sadie You could lick the tables.

Kyla You could lick the floor.

Sadie Yeah you could . . . do it.

Pause.

Kyla Wha?

Sadie Go on, I'll give you twenty quid.

Kyla No.

Sadie I dare you.

Kyla Fuck that.

Sadie It will be a laugh.

Kyla I'm not licking the floor.

Sadie . . .

Kyla You can't be serious?

She hesitates, then kneels down to lick the floor.

Cheney *enters.*

Cheney What the hell are you doing on the floor?

They both laugh.

Ruby *enters out of breath.*

Ruby Don't take those things from me Sadie.

Sadie We're messing with you.

Kyla Your face! Yer sweating.

Ruby Coz I bloody pegged it yer.

Kyla You live across the road, if you spat it would hit the shop.

Cheney Do you want anything Ruby?

Ruby How kind of you to ask.

Cheney Dun be cheeky.

Ruby Just wings, I'm starving.

Sadie Put it on my tab.

Ruby Aw thanks Sadez.

Sadie Sadie.

Ruby Soz.

She gives her a big hug.

Cheney Right girls, I'm just popping upstairs to the flat to/

Kyla We don't care.

Cheney Well I was just saying.

Kyla Well don't just say.

Sadie We'll hold the fort.

Cheney I'm sure you will.

Cheney *leaves.*

Ruby You OK?

Sadie She's fine. We've been talking about you.

Ruby Kyla been slagging me off again?

Sadie No, we were praising you actually.

Kyla Yeah praise be.

Sadie So /

Kyla Shit! My phone died. Ruby, did you bring your charger?

Ruby No.

Kyla Fuck my life, I feel like I'm dying without my phone.

Sadie It's been twenty seconds. You know when I was your age I didn't have a phone.

Ruby Woah that's mad in-it?

Sadie No one sat around watching naff videos of mums in Asda talking about milk.

Kyla Ruby loves all that.

Sadie Grocery hauls are so fucking boring.

Kyla Some spring onions, some kiwis, some tomatoes, some lemons, some bread, some oats, some fibre tablets for my weak bowels and then all the tins in the tinned aisle BECAUSE THE WORLD IS ENDING AND I'M BORED AND CAN'T LIVE WITHOUT MY FUCKING PHONE!

Pause.

Sadie Woah . . . you really are bored. I've got a game for us.

Kyla A game?

Sadie This is what we did when I was your age.

She gets three cans of pop and opens them, getting the girls to sit at a table.

Ruby   And what is your age Sadie?

Kyla   How old are dinosaurs, Sadez?

Sadie   Rude! It's Sadie! You're getting too chopsy you.

Kyla   Yeah yeah what's this game then?

Sadie   Have you ever played, 'Never Have I Ever'?

Ruby   Nope.

Kyla   Yeah, course.

Ruby   I'm shit at games.

Sadie   You can't lose with this one. Usually I play it with straight vodka.

Kyla   So basically Rub you/

Sadie   I'm telling the rules!

Kyla   Oh, OK.

Sadie   So, this is how it goes. Someone makes a statement about something and you swig if you have and if you haven't you don't. For example, never have I ever nicked from Superdrug?

They all drink.

We're all thieves.

Kyla   Some things are just meant to be stolen.

Ruby   Who can afford lip gloss?

Sadie   You're turn chopsy.

Beat.

Kyla   Never have I ever pinched money from my dad.

They all drink.

Sadie   Never have I ever fingered myself.

Kyla *and* **Sadie** *drink.*

Kyla Never have I ever given someone a blowie.

Kyla and **Sadie** *drink.*

Sadie C'mon Rub join in.

Ruby I dun /

Sadie Join in.

She makes **Kyla** *chant with her.*

Sadie/Kyla RUBY. RUBY. RUBY. RUBY. RUBY.

Ruby OK!

Pause.

Never have I ever kicked a pigeon.

Kyla A pigeon? . . .

Ruby He deserved it for being a pigeon.

Kyla You were dropped on your head at birth you swear to god.

Sadie Kyla drink or don't drink, don't be a cow about it.

Kyla, Sadie *and* **Ruby** *drink.*

Sadie Never have I ever kissed someone.

They all drink.

Kyla You ain't kissed anyone.

Ruby I have?

Kyla When?

Ruby Um /

Kyla She hasn't kissed anyone with tongues Sadie.

Ruby I have.

Kyla You haven't coz if you had you'd be chewing my ear off about it.

Sadie   Leave her be!

Sadie *hugs* **Ruby**.

Sadie   Have you never kissed anyone before Ruby?

Ruby   I'm not bothered.

Sadie   Everyone is bothered.

Kyla   Yeah everyone's bothered.

Sadie   Come here.

Ruby   What?

Sadie   It's the most natural thing in the world.

Ruby   . . .

Sadie   Do you want my help or not?

Ruby   I do it's just I don't wanna kiss you, no offence.

Kyla   That's offensive to be fair.

Sadie   Girls kiss girls sometimes it's no big deal. It's just practicing.

Kyla   Yeah Rub don't be homophobic.

Ruby   I'm not.

Kyla *laughs*.

Kyla   She hasn't got a clue.

Sadie   Why don't you kiss her then.

Kyla   NO WAY!

Sadie   Shut your face then.

Sadie *leans in and kisses* **Ruby**.

Kyla *looks on*.

It lingers for too long and then **Sadie** *pulls away*.

Sadie   You were great.

Sadie *laughs which makes* **Ruby** *laugh.*

Ruby Was I?

Sadie My god you've got great bone structure.

Ruby Really?

Sadie Exquisite.

Pause.

You know what, let's get some pictures. Get on the table.

Kyla *obediently gets on the table.*

Ruby's *reluctant.*

Sadie C' mon Ruby.

Kyla *gets on the table.*

Sadie Pretend yer someone else.

Kyla Like who?

Sadie Someone you think is powerful and sexy.

Ruby Like Beyoncé.

Kyla Kehlani.

Ruby Charli XCX.

Sadie Whatever floats yer boat. Come on Ruby?!

Kyla *happily poses.*

Ruby *looks out of her depth but gets on the table.*

Sadie C'mon Ruby.

She puts them into suggestive positions.

OK I think this looks great. Are we ready?

Kyla Yeah.

Ruby . . .

Sadie ... THREE, TWO, ONE ... HOT CHICKS!

Kyla/Ruby HOT CHICKS.

Kyla Filter the shit out of that Sadez.

Sadie Sadie.

Kyla Soz.

Sadie OK we're gonna do a glow up.

Kyla I've always wanted some filler for my lips.

Sadie No on your TikToks.

Ruby I'm happy with mine as it is.

Sadie Yours looks childish.

Ruby Bu I /

Sadie Let's sort your feed out.

Kyla I'm down.

Sadie Men love a sexy vid.

Kyla They knock one out over it.

Sadie You've seen mine.

She shows them hers, it's sexy and suggestive but feels highbrow at the same time.

Ruby Bu /

Sadie Give it here I'll sort it.

Sadie *snatches the phone off her and starts looking at her profile.*

You need to get rid of this, this, defo this, and OK ... I've got a lot more relevant content of you. I'll sort it.

Kyla What about me?

Sadie I'll sort you next. Let's find us some real men.

Scene Five

Loyalty/*Teyrngarwch*

Ruby *is doing a TikTok video and trying to get* **Cheney** *to join in.*

Kyla *is engrossed in her phone, she is dressed exactly like* **Sadie** *in the previous scene and is not impressed by their antics.*

Ruby   Aw c'mon Chen lets see your moves.

Cheney   I used to throw some serious shapes in Time and Envy back in the day I tell you.

Ruby   Well lets see them then.

She tries to record him.

Ruby   Shake yer arse Chen.

Cheney   Stop recording me.

She's recording him.

Ruby   I'm not.

Cheney   Yer recording my bum in-you. Please don't do that without my consent. Thank you.

She's recording his arse shaking.

Ruby   Shake yer booty.

Cheney   Tell her Kyla.

Kyla   I ain't got time for your childish videos anymore.

Ruby   It's not childish.

Kyla   It is and we don't do that anymore.

Ruby   Don't we?

Kyla   No.

She goes to show her their TikTok but **Kyla** *throws* **Ruby**'s *phone across the floor.*

Ruby   Oi.

Cheney Was that necessary you could have broken it and those phones are expensive.

Kyla Is it broken?

Ruby No . . . thankfully.

Kyla There we go then. I'd have just bought her a new one anyway.

Cheney Stop boasting money bags.

Kyla Get me a coffee.

Cheney Milk?

Kyla Black.

Cheney Coming up.

Cheney *leaves.*

Kyla She's late. She's never late.

Ruby Probably in Ibiza . . . or dead.

Kyla For fuck sake why ain't she answering!

Ruby Sometimes she ghosts though, doesn't she? Says it's her downtime. Like when she went to Santorini.

Beat.

Kyla Well she still spoke with me.

Ruby It sounded like a magical place Santorini.

Kyla We FaceTimed every night.

Ruby Don't you think its nice having a few days off running?

Kyla No.

Ruby Coz yer nan's started noticing shit ain't she and /

Kyla Don't worry I've sorted her.

Ruby Have you?

Kyla I gave her five hundred quid to shut her up. She bought an air fryer, and some fags so she's happy like. It dented my savings but my choice.

Ruby Didn't she ask what you were doing to make the money?

Kyla She just said the less she asks about where it's from the better. Anyway, I can do what I want with my money. We'll make more money if we carry on. It will benefit Nan in the long run. Why are you being neggy?

Beat.

Ruby I'm not.

Kyla You're like a running machine Rub.

Ruby Am I?

Kyla Yer like the queen of drug running, you're well good at it.

Ruby I don't wanna be.

Kyla Even Sadie said to me the other day how great you are at it.

Ruby Do you think we should stop?

Kyla We're nearly at our Vegas target and we need a holiday.

Ruby Yeah I don't think I wanna go there anymore.

Kyla Why not?

Ruby I just think its a bit far and/

Kyla . . .

Ruby Like the other week when you got smacked in the face by that guy who was off his tits and /

Kyla That was rare, we don't normally deal with low-life fucks bu, Sadie got someone to fuck the guy up for touching me so, she's got our backs.

Ruby I don't want to go to prison.

Kyla We're not gonna go to prison, we're not old enough.

Ruby But it's scary and I think we should /

Kyla *starts counting some money out of an envelope.*

Kyla Pass me your cut to give to Sadie.

Ruby *looks blank.*

Kyla Pass me yer money so it's ready for when she gets yer.

Beat.

Ruby Ky? Don't lose yer head righ?

Kyla Wha?

Ruby Don't.

Kyla Just bloody say it will you!

Ruby See you're losing your head /

Kyla OK JUST FUCKING SAY!

Silence.

Ruby Dad took the money this week.

Kyla You wha /

Ruby I'm sorry.

Kyla That's like 6K. Yer suppose to keep tabs.

Ruby I know.

Kyla You've been told to keep the money on you at all times.

Ruby I'm really sorry.

Scene Five

Kyla You're gonna be in so much shit.

Ruby Shit.

Kyla She's gonna go postal. You're so stupid.

Ruby Don't say that.

Kyla Well it's true.

Ruby We could use some of our Vegas savings and she'd never have to know.

Kyla I'm not cleaning up your shit.

Ruby But Ky /

Kyla I'm not doing it.

Ruby Don't be like this /

She goes to touch **Kyla** *but she shoves her back hard.*

Cheney *enters.*

Cheney What you pair rowing bou?

Kyla *storms out of the shop on her phone.*

Ruby's *phone pings with a load of dick pics.*

Ruby She's obsessed with her.

Cheney Who?

Ruby Sadie.

Ruby's *phone pings – dick pics,* **Cheney** *sees it.*

Cheney Are those /

Ruby Keep away from me.

Cheney Why have you got pictures of men's bits on your phone?

Ruby Keep out my fucking business.

Cheney Don't speak like that to me.

Ruby You're a pervert.

Cheney Ruby! Do you wanna tell me what's going on?

Sadie *walks in with* **Kyla**.

Sadie Can I get some chicken please Chen?

Cheney I'll put it on your tab.

Cheney *begins boxing some chicken.*

Sadie Yer so sweet.

She points to the girls to sit opposite her on a table.

Cheney They've been squabbling.

Sadie I heard, we need to bang their heads together.

Cheney Do you want some chicken girls?

Sadie They've had enough.

Cheney *sets the box down in front of* **Sadie**.

Sadie Give us five Chen.

Cheney Sure . . . Everything OK?

Beat.

Sadie Yeah all fine. Just, girl chat.

Cheney Oh that will be too much for me.

Beat.

Sadie Thanks.

Cheney *goes out the back.*

Sadie *opens a box of chicken.*

Kyla I had nothing to do with it.

Ruby Sadez I /

Sadie SADIE!

Pause.

She passes the chicken to **Kyla**.

Kyla I'm not hungry.

Sadie Don't be ungrateful eat it.

Kyla *starts to eat the wing.*

Sadie You're grown women. Do you get that? The system is broken and we need to play it. Everything is accountable. Every single action has consequences.

Kyla *puts the bones down on the counter having eaten the chicken.*

Sadie Do you know how much flavour is in there? . . . Eat it.

Kyla *begins gnawing at the bone of the chicken.*

Sadie I need that money back.

Ruby I'll get it back for you.

Sadie Yer father will have pissed it away by now.

Kyla She can use our savings.

Sadie You shouldn't suffer for her stupidity.

Ruby Don't call me stupid.

Kyla *puts the bone down.*

Sadie Keep eating. This is my work. Something I've built up over years of hard graft and I won't stop until I get to where I'm supposed to be. I want you to be by my side Ruby when I do it.

Kyla What about me?

Beat.

Kyla We will make it up to you.

Beat.

We can mend it, please?

She leaves.

Kyla *begins to pace.*

Kyla Why do you always fuck things up?

Ruby . . .

Kyla Answer me.

Ruby Some guy threatened to kill me on a drop off the other day.

Kyla So.

Ruby I could have died.

Kyla Well you didn't.

Ruby You've been smashed in the face.

Kyla I dun care.

Ruby We got chased through Uplands the other day and had to hide in a bin.

Kyla I do remember I was there.

Ruby Well its . . . its getting too much and I dun think /

Kyla Wha?

Ruby Well I dun think Sadie cares that much.

Kyla She gives us compensation when that happens so it's no biggie.

Ruby But what if /

Kyla I dun wanna hear this.

Ruby Kyla.

Kyla Just give me space to fucking think!

Ruby . . .

The girls' phones ping at the same time – a voice note from **Sadie***.*

Kyla *plays the voice note.*

Sadie Look girls, I put a lot of pressure on myself to make this successful. I need to know you are on my side and, even though no one ever gave me a second chance I'm gonna give you one. So don't waste it. I'll meet you at Cheney's Friday at eight. I need you to dress up. You can buy it out of your savings. It's the least you can do for me. I've got a big deal with an epic payout and if I pull it off I'll give you 2K each.

The voice note finishes.

Ruby Do we really have to do this?

Kyla You owe me Ruby.

Ruby *sends her a voice note.*

Ruby . . . Hey . . . Sadie . . . We're /

Sadie *lingers by the door.*

Kyla YOU!

Ruby . . . I'm . . . really sorry about my dad. I'd like to make it up to you . . . I'll make it up to both of you.

Silence.

Sadie You better.

Scene Six

Claws/*Crafangau*

Kyla *and* **Ruby** *are dressed in party gear, they look older than they have done in previous scenes.*

Cheney *is restocking.*

Cheney Where are you off?

Kyla . . . Church.

Cheney Looking like that?

Kyla God loves everyone.

Cheney I highly doubt he loves everyone.

Kyla Everyone.

Cheney Murderers?

Kyla Yep.

Cheney Rapists?

Kyla Even paedos.

Cheney What about /

Kyla For fucks sake Chen who gives a shit.

Beat.

Cheney You got a right nastiness about you today.

Kyla Yeah yeah.

He looks at **Ruby**.

Cheney You OK Ruby?

Kyla Keep your beak out.

Cheney You're a bully Kyla.

She wanders up to him and throws a twenty pound note in his face.

Kyla Get us two Diet Cokes . . . and keep the change.

He goes out the back to get the cans.

Kyla Yer gonna be OK.

Ruby I don't look like me do I?

Kyla You look better.

Ruby I feel like I'm gonna be sick.

Kyla You don't, it's all in yer head.

Cheney *returns with the Diet Cokes.*

Cheney Your nan came in for chips earlier and said you weren't in school again.

Kyla Little tell-tale tit.

Cheney She's worried about you.

Kyla Yeah sure she is. Anyway, it's Ruby who's been suspended. I'm just not turning up in solidarity.

Cheney You've been suspended?

Kyla For not coming in.

Cheney Where's the sense in that?

Kyla We dun need school, we're making bank our own way.

Cheney Coz you still ain't reached 100K followers.

Kyla You don't give a shit, none of you do so we're sorting ourselves out. Got to take the world, it won't be handed to you and that's what we're doing.

He goes back to cleaning.

Ruby I think I should get back to look after Dad.

Kyla What for? That dick deserves to die.

Ruby Don't say that. We were down A&E waiting for twelve hours. I was scared he was gonna bleed to death.

Kyla Serves him right.

Ruby They took the money, well what was left. I told you this is dangerous.

Kyla It wasn't his money he shouldn't have taken it in the first place.

Beat.

Ruby I think she did it.

Kyla What?

Ruby I think Sadie did it.

Kyla Jumped him? Behave!

Ruby I think she got people to do it but I think it was her.

Kyla Don't start chatting shit now she's on her way.

Ruby . . .

Kyla Keep your trap shut.

Ruby I don't get why we have to dress up like this.

Kyla Don't ask too many questions.

Ruby I won't.

Kyla Coz yer already in her shit books.

Ruby I texted her sorry like a hundred times.

Kyla She said if we pull this off she'll give us 2K each and it will cover what you lost.

Cheney *starts wiping tables.*

Cheney Do you want any chips girls?

Kyla No.

Ruby I don't feel well.

Kyla Think about how much money we're gonna earn. We're gonna smash the Vegas fund.

Sadie *glides in looking a billion bucks.*

Cheney Coffee to go?

Sadie Yes.

Cheney I can use my new coffee machine you bought me.

Sadie Ledge.

He goes out the back.

She sits down at the table opposite **Ruby** *and* **Kyla**.

Sadie You both need to lose the puffas.

Ruby But it's cold.

Sadie They look childish.

Kyla Where are we going then?

Sadie A big party.

Kyla Great, we're gonna get up to our tits aren't we? Lush.

Sadie No.

Beat.

We're working. We're always working. Got that?

Beat.

Kyla Yeah.

Beat.

Sadie Ready to go?

Ruby . . . About that I'm not feeling too good.

Sadie You'll be fine once we get there.

Ruby But I feel really /

Sadie *presents a baggie to* **Ruby**.

Sadie Take this.

Ruby No.

Sadie Here. Sniff.

She opens the baggie, takes **Ruby**'s *finger then sticks it in the baggie then shoves it in her mouth.*

Sadie You'll come up in a bit and feel a hundred times better.

She tries to snatch the bag but **Sadie** *won't let her.*

Kyla Where's the party?

Sadie The Mumbles. Big posh house we have clientele there. You just need to get them on their own and do the drop offs.

Ruby But we don't normally speak to them we just /

Kyla Jesus well this time we are.

Sadie's *phone rings and she goes to answer it outside.*

Ruby But what if something goes wrong?

Kyla What's gonna go wrong?

Ruby I dunno just /

Kyla I'm gonna be there. I won't let anything happen to you.

Ruby But what if /

Kyla YER RATTLING ME MUN!

Silence.

Sadie *comes back in.*

Sadie OK change of plan.

Kyla What?

Sadie Only Ruby's coming now.

Ruby No. I don't want to.

Kyla Wha? That's not fair.

Sadie They don't want two kids wandering around.

Kyla Kids?

Sadie You know what I mean.

Kyla You told us to dress older so do we not look old enough?

She takes a long hard look.

Sadie You look try hard to be honest.

Scene Six 65

Kyla What the fuck?

Sadie Come on Ruby, we need to get going.

Ruby Bu /

Kyla I look older than Ruby. This is mental.

Sadie We don't need you.

Ruby I don't want to go on my own.

Sadie You'll be with me.

Ruby I don't want to go without Ky.

Sadie We can't be late.

Sadie *goes to get* **Ruby** *up.*

Sadie GET THE FUCK UP NOW!

Ruby I don't like going anywhere without Kyla.

Sadie (*mocking*)   Are you too scared to do anything without Kyla?

Sadie *laughs and prompts* **Kyla** *to laugh along.*

Sadie Don't be so stupid.

Beat.

Ruby I'm not stupid.

Sadie You owe me for that money your dad stole.

Ruby Well you got it back in the end because you jumped my dad.

Kyla Ruby, I told you not to bring that up.

Ruby My dad had to get his skull glued back together.

Sadie Don't be so dramatic it was just a little kicking.

Ruby How could you do that /

Sadie Because he deserved it the low-life fuck.

Sadie *takes the baggie and dabs some on her gums and tongue.*

She needs to come with me or the deal is off.

Kyla Just do what she says.

Beat.

Ruby Please can she come with us? I don't want any more money.

Sadie Kyla is staying here.

Ruby No!

Sadie We're supposed to be a team.

Ruby I don't want to go without you.

Sadie If you want to be childish about this I'll find some other girls who will take me up on my /

Kyla RUBY GO!

Silence.

She reluctantly walks out and **Sadie** *follows.*

Sadie Stay here.

She leaves.

Cheney *comes out with the coffee.*

Cheney She forgot her coffee. I ground the beans to make it proper like and /

Kyla I don't think she cares.

Cheney Where've they gone?

Kyla Oh who gives a fuck.

She puts her feet up on the table and begins scrolling her phone.

Cheney Maybe if you were a nicer girl she would have taken you. Ever thought about that?

He begins cleaning down tables.

Scene Seven

Bite/*Brathiad*

Later that evening.

For the first time, **Cheney** *is sitting down, taking a brief break.*

Kyla *is on her phone.*

Cheney Do you know I've never got the appeal.

Kyla . . .

Cheney Phones like, no one looks at each other anymore. No one talks and it all just makes you sad.

Kyla . . . That's the world now.

Cheney I know I know. What's happening with Vegas then?

Kyla Dunno.

Cheney It's overrated anyway.

Kyla How would you know?

Cheney Coz I've been there.

Beat.

Kyla What? Never said.

Cheney I mean, I went in the 90s when I drove from San Jose through the Death Valley to Nevada and /

Kyla Don't need a geography sesh.

Cheney To get to Vegas . . . and in the desert sun it's tiring and cheap. But at night it's glamorous and dangerous. No place for young women.

Silence.

Kyla I'm done with Ruby. She's an arse-hat.

Cheney You dun mean that.

Kyla I do.

She begins to sweep.

Cheney Aw, see yer a nice girl deep down in-you?

Kyla Yeah, dun tell anyone will you?

Cheney Brownies' honour.

Kyla Yeah like they had you in the Brownies.

He gives her a knowing wink and walks out the back. She continues sweeping stuff into the bin.

Ruby *walks in, blood running down her legs.*

Kyla Shit Rub . . . How long have you been standing there? Did you turn off your phone? I bet it was a shit party. Are you gonna say sorry to me? If you carry on I'll do what I did to Holly. I binned her no messing . . . Why are you looking like that?

Ruby I'd done two drop offs.

The kitchen.

A downstairs toilet.

Then Sadie.

She said.

Utility room.

Wasn't sure what that was.

She laughed.

Said it's where the washing machine is.

I thought.

To have a whole room just for washing.

And it smelt like.

Clean clothes.

He closed the door.

They don't normally say much but he.

Was.

Chatty.

And close.

His breath stunk.

Skin was rough.

Smell of clean washing.

Dryer on.

He'd blocked the door.

Shoved my knickers.

To the side.

I.

I didn't want.

To let him.

Bu.

He kept going and.

I knew.

I had to go.

Through with it.

Like you said.

Just get it done.

He made a big noise.

Sounded like . . .

I turned to look.

He started to cry.

I ran and ran back yer . . .

I was bleeding.

Embarrassed and.

And d'you know what I was thinking . . .

The day she left . . .

Jilly stormed out . . .

Something in her voice.

Made me . . .

She meant it.

So I went for her leg.

Clung on tight and without even.

Looking down . . .

She just kicked me.

Off her like I was nothing.

You said I didn't need a mam.

You didn't have one . . .

And you were . . .

You were just fine.

You said all we needed was.

Each other . . .

You didn't believe that though did you?

We'd argue, you'd drag Jilly up and shout.

Shout.

SHOUT! . . .

She left because I always.

Fucked things up.

I deserved it.

Because I'm stupid and.

She couldn't hack it could she?

Mam couldn't handle me.

You though, you could.

You called me stupid, just like he said I was.

I've never known.

What it's like to feel safe.

Like proper.

Tuck you up in bed.

Safe.

Not with Jilly.

Not with you and.

Kyla Ruby I /

Ruby I, I, I should . . .

Kyla Ruby please /

Ruby I fucking should with you. Shouldn't I Ky?

Sadie *walks into the shop.*

Sadie Ruby, why did you run off like that? I was getting us an Uber.

Kyla She's bleeding.

Sadie She's finally come on haven't you Rub?

Sadie *hands* **Ruby** *a bunch of serviettes from a table.*

Sadie Shove these in your knickers. I always do this when I'm caught short.

Ruby's *frozen.*

Sadie Do you want me to do it, come here.

She kneels down to put the serviettes in her knickers but **Ruby** *steps back.*

Sadie Well go do it yourself then. Chop chop.

Ruby *wanders into the toilet.*

Sadie Why are you looking at me like that?

Silence.

Kyla Did you let someone touch her?

Sadie Jealous are you?

Kyla No, of course I'm not.

Sadie Did you want to fuck her instead?

Kyla You're disgusting.

Beat.

Sadie *laughs.*

Sadie Look please don't get involved in my business.

Kyla We need to get her to a hospital.

Kyla *starts banging on the toilet door.*

C'mon Ruby we need to get you to somewhere to get looked at and /

Sadie She's not going anywhere.

Kyla Ruby?! You need to . . . Please. Please. Please! Just fucking . . . listen /

Cheney *comes out to see what the commotion is.*

Cheney What's going on here?

Sadie Can you give us a minute?

Kyla No, I want him to hear all this. We want the money that's owed to us and we want you to never come back here.

Sadie Don't make me laugh.

Kyla We want what was promised. You owe us.

Sadie I think it's the other way around.

Kyla How?

Sadie You guys owe me 50K.

Cheney 50K?

Sadie Yeah, when am I going to get that back?

Cheney How do you owe her all that?

Sadie Clothes, makeup, skincare/

Kyla You were throwing them out.

Sadie Chicken. Loads of chicken. Like a pair of little spongers you've been.

Kyla DON'T CALL ME A SPONGER!

Cheney Let's all just cool it down a bit.

Sadie Keep out of this!

Cheney *steps back*.

Sadie You two are just a pair of fucking spongers!

Kyla You call us spongers but it's you who leaches the life out of anyone that gets in your way. Who'd want to be around a poisonous criminal like you?

Sadie Well you'll be in the cell next to me babe.

Kyla Yeah, bu at least I ain't a paedophile.

Pause.

Sadie Don't chat shit you don't understand.

Kyla Sticking your old dinosaur tongue down a child's gob/

Sadie Stop talking.

Kyla Sticking your tongue down a child's gob. Taking pictures for your wank bank of kids.

Sadie Stop fucking talking now!

Kyla Paedophile. I bet you wanted to fuck her and film it and send to other paedos at that party and/

Sadie Do you know I wanted to choose you? But that was so stupid. Coz you. You're the one who's a liability, a fuck up who's not going anywhere coz you can't keep in line. You just talk, talk, FUCKING TALK and it's got you in trouble now hasn't it? It's all your fault.

Kyla WE'RE JUST KIDS!

Sharp pause.

Sadie *grabs her and starts to strangle her.*

They tussle and **Cheney** *tries to break them up.*

Ruby *comes out.*

Ruby *tries to push* **Kyla** *away from* **Sadie**.

Ruby STOP! WE NEED TO STOP!!!

Ruby *pushes* **Kyla** *too hard.*

Kyla *falls back on the floor knocked out cold.*

EVERYTHING STOPS!

Sadie You do anything, I'll ring the police and tell them you've been fucking the girls in the back alley. You mark my words, they take one look at you and they'll think you're a paedo.

Pause.

Sadie Everyone around here knows you're an odd bod and you act like a paedophile so who are they gonna believe? You? Or a woman?

Ruby . . . Is she OK?

Beat.

Sadie You have to come with me.

Ruby . . . Where?

Cheney *goes towards* **Kyla**.

Cheney We can't just leave her.

Sadie Don't!

Beat.

Ruby I love her.

Sadie She didn't give a fuck about you and look what's happened. The only person you should give a fuck about now is yourself.

Sadie *gets her phone out and calls someone.*

I need you to do a swift pick up . . . I'll send you my location . . . Within the hour?

She puts the phone down and looks at **Ruby**.

Sadie This is the world now . . . it's ugly and savage. But you'll grow stronger. I'll help you grow stronger.

She holds out her hand to **Ruby**.

Sadie You've got me now.

Ruby *takes her hand.*

Ruby *takes one more look at* **Kyla**.

She exits with **Sadie**.

Cheney *kneels beside* **Kyla** *holding her hand.*

Scene Eight

Chicks/Cywion

A year later.

A shop sits in the middle of a parade of shops, 'CHENEY'S CHICKEN'. The shop is tired, but as clean as a takeout joint could be.

Cheney *sets down two boxes of chicken in front of* **Sadie**.

Ruby *enters looking exactly like* **Sadie**.

Cheney *hands over the coffee to* **Sadie** *then lingers.*

He reluctantly leaves.

Ruby *and* **Sadie** *sit together for a while.*

Sadie *hands over a big wedge of money to* **Ruby**.

She puts it in her pocket and **Sadie** *leaves.*

Ruby *settles into position and adjusts the chicken boxes on the table.*

She hears the distant din of the girls coming up the street.

She hears the door open

She looks up, smiles and then –

Blackout/Tywyllwch.

For a complete listing of
Methuen Drama titles, visit:
www.bloomsbury.com/drama

Follow us on Twitter and keep up to date
with our news and publications
@MethuenDrama